D0612709

MT
1
.G475
R5

DATE DUE

██████			
		OCT 3 0 2002	

Demco, Inc. 38-293

PRINTED IN U.S.A.   23-364-002

Rhythm, Reason and Response

Rhythm, Reason and Response

For the Musician, Pianist and Teacher

Irene A. Glasford

AN EXPOSITION–UNIVERSITY BOOK

EXPOSITION PRESS   NEW YORK

EXPOSITION PRESS INC.

50 Jericho Turnpike   Jericho, New York 1175?

FIRST EDITION

© 1970 by Irene A. Glasford. *All rights reserved, including the right of reproduction in whole or in part in any form except for short quotations in critical essays and reviews.* Manufactured in the United States of America.

LIBRARY OF CONGRESS CATALOG CARD NUMBER: 76-126367

0-682-47113-5

MT
.G475
R5

Contents

1-30622

Acknowledgments

Nothing that has been written in a vacuum can have value, for one of the more significant measures of a work is its degree of relevance to human experience. Another such measure is the degree to which one has researched, discovered, considered, and creatively applied the thoughts of others to one's own efforts. Accordingly, I would like to express my gratitude to the following people, who are so much a part of this book:

—To Gertrude H. Murdough, the eminent piano teacher with whom I have had the privilege of studying, and whose vision and creativity have been a continual inspiration;

—To Cora Belle Hunter, who introduced me to the principles of Mabel Elsworth Todd, and who helped me to see that Miss Todd's principles might be applied to all forms of physical movement, especially as they apply to her concept of total rhythm;

—To Dr. Frederick Schlieder, who believed so fervently in the divine nature of music and in the role of creative improvisation as a part of the musical experience;

—To Dr. Guy Maier, who was in the finest sense of the expression a "musician at heart," and who offered me endless encouragement;

—To Helen Vietmeier and Claudia Beier, who have urged me to define my approach to music in written form.

In addition, I wish to thank Judith Cochran Carlberg, who has helped me to organize and to write this book. To my students who have helped me crystallize and vivify my approach to music, to the many authors and publishers who have allowed me to incorporate their material into this book, and to Frances Taylor, who is responsible for the drawings in this volume, I am deeply indebted.

Lastly, I am grateful to my husband, who has patiently watched the development of this work from its beginnings to fruition.

Preface

Today's private piano teacher may or may not perform publicly, and may or may not consider it necessary to prepare his students for performance beyond their own enjoyment. Such a teacher probably seeks reassurance in an occasional seminar where he hears gifted students perform, airs and compares problems of technique in his field, acquires a new list of publications to bolster his repertoire, and relates and clarifies pianistic processes and interpretations of compositions. He learns to depend on the innate musical talent of gifted students, on the imitation of himself, on the recordings and live performances of artists, and on traditional terminology and poetic imagery to bridge the gap between academic drilling and the living musical experience.

Upon returning home from such seminars, the private piano teacher earns a living, answers his community's growing need for musical instruction, and seldom has the time to reflect on what constitutes the difference between the playing of his gifted students and that of his less-than-gifted students. It is precisely this gap between the artistic performance and the less-than-total musical experience, however, that he *should* examine, as a help both to himself and to the perplexed student who finds that taking music lessons is very different from the experience of music as he first heard and delighted in it.

Because of the limited time that the music teacher may spend with each student, he finds it difficult to get outside or to go beyond the realm of purely academic teaching. Certain elements, such as the response to symbols, the development of pianistic patterns, and basic theory, must be taught. Since any of these elements requires some time for mastery or for even partial comprehension, months and often years elapse before the student is exposed to the spiritual-creative-emotional wholeness of music. There is little time for the teacher to cultivate the intrinsic creativity that most individuals, through their experience with the universal elements of sound and motion, bring to their first music lesson.

It is undeniable that rudimentary training for the beginning student is necessary; however, it is equally true that such drills and exercises tend to destroy the exuberance with which most children (and adults, too) greet their first musical experience. The disillusioning gap between the vital musical experience and the day-by-day drudgery of drill after drill is often not bridged, not because of the teacher's unwillingness to give more of himself, but because music requires care in the mastery of symbols and patterns. Discouragement thus conquers the first bloom of enthusiasm, and the project of learning and living music is hastily abandoned. The student's vision of his goal dims.

The important realization for both the drill-conscious teacher and the frustrated student is that beyond and transcending these often loathsome but wholly necessary training exercises lies the unseen world of creativity and musical fulfillment. Beyond the endless labors of repetition, there is a goal worth our commitment and pursuit. It is the attainment of this goal that so often constitutes the difference between the gifted and the average piano student, or between the inspired concert pianist and a pianist who has perfect technical mastery but little else.

I propose that the basic difference between the gifted artist (not necessarily one who plays professionally) and the less-than-gifted performer is that the former, through his synthesis of music, mind, body, and feeling, is effortlessly employing laws of motion which consistently occur in nature. This synthesizing process is sensed in a total rhythm which we call the "carrying-line." Many books have been written on one or the other of the aforementioned topics, but to my knowledge no one has written previously of:

1. the musician stimulated through aural images, his body, his breathing, and the music itself, as these are synthesized *as one process in a total rhythm;*
2. the awareness of the breath as energy, vitality, power, and rhythm;

3. the awakening and potential creativity of total rhythm through kinesthesia;*

4. the awakening and stimulating of the kinesthetic awareness until habit replaces mere symbols and until the performer becomes the channel through which music is released.

It is my intention to demonstrate that each of these is integral to the complete musical experience.

Any pianist who is less than a genius (and this category includes most of us!) requires a means that will allow him not only to acquire technical competence, but also to approach the inspired performance of the artist. Although no system is universally accepted as being better than any other, there is a valuable approach which originates with the concept that any natural movement is cyclical and therefore complete.

Rather than attempt to create still another logical "system" for playing musical instruments in general and the piano in particular, I will instead outline my approach to music. This approach, of course, demands different terminology, an inclusive technique unifying inner spirit and outer mechanics, and imagery relating to body, rhythm, and dynamics. These principles remain the same for all students from ages four to ninety; the teacher, however, can clarify the experience by developing images appropriate to each. The inventive teacher may employ imagination, imagery, and kinesthesia in teaching these concepts; and the student must practice and actually "live" the approach until the necessary habits are ingrained.

I am writing essentially because I have seen and heard so many nearly gifted piano students who, with a set of basic, natural, universal principles to guide them, might have approached greatness. Unfortunately, many students have been allowed to scatter their energies on a fragmented, piecemeal, quasi-musical philosophy. The purpose of this book, therefore, is to synthesize the fragmentary welter of principles into a totally cohesive and understandable whole.

---

* See glossary.

I. The Balanced Skeletal Structure and the Total Performance

> . . . the human body has not its symmetrical design because the law of beauty requires such a design. It has its symmetrical design merely for functional demands. . . . ."balance" is the primary idea. . . .[1]

> The way you balance your bones and use them determines your degree of self-possession and command of your forces.[2]

Critics have said of the actress Eleonora Duse that her art is essentially spiritual. I would respond that even though her message may be spiritual, her physical body most certainly is the medium for that message.

Along a similar line, while having a lesson with Dr. Guy Maier, I was asked to change the dynamics of a particular interpretation. After I made my alterations, Dr. Maier remarked, "What on earth are you thinking, that you can gather control so quickly? Whatever it is, go ahead, organize it, and teach it, because it works."

As the body serves as the medium for Eleonora Duse's art, so it was entirely accountable for the change in dynamics in Dr. Maier's studio. For all artists and would-be pianists, the importance of the body is undeniable. To free it for its function as the vehicle for music expression, it is imperative that one have an understanding of its components, structure, function, limitations, and possibilities.

---

[1] Eliel Saarinen, *Search for Form: A Fundamental Approach to Art* (New York, 1948), pp. 284-285.

[2] Mabel Elsworth Todd, *The Hidden You: What You Are and What to Do about It* (New York, 1953), p. 71.

For the pianist, the spine is the basis of support and movement for the entire body. In addition to serving as a nerve center and message relay station, the strongest sections of the spine are largely responsible for the strength of the arms and legs. In its connective capacity, the spine joins the pelvis (the pianist's base of support) with the rib case and head. The head sits, the ribs hang, and the pelvis is braced on the spine. Because there is no bone in the abdominal wall, no weight travels downward through the front of the body if the abdominal wall is functioning properly.

Of particular interest to all musicians is the fact that the spine is a vertical plane. Its role is self-evident in the poise and performance of the more controlled pianist such as Wilhelm Kempf, Artur Rubinstein, or Lili Krauss, whose mannerisms in no way becloud the sincerity of their musical output. Under the most favorable conditions, the head and spine function as a single, balanced unit in a straight but flexible line. An imaginary line passes through the center of the blocks of weight represented by the head, the rib case, and the pelvis.

Conceived in this manner, there are "two forces" or directional energies in the body that become immediately apparent. One of these extends downward from the head through the spine to the bench (the "mechanical force"); the other extends upward from the bench toward the head (the "living force"). In the ideal condition, this pull to the earth ("down energy") and push upward ("up energy") will be in balance. To maintain a light stability, the pianist must "think down the back and up the front."

The portion of the body that centers and balances these forces is the spine. The anterior of the body is suspended from the spine and head. It is common knowledge that the longer the axis of a flexible, curved structure controlling weight (the spine in this case), the closer the weights are to center balance and the greater the speed and power of movement. These principles will be further clarified for the pianist in later pages.

Allegorically, the flexible, curving spine may be understood as a long, rhythmic line. Ideally the pianist keeps the "line" intact but not rigid. This ideal is only infrequently the case, however, and the line of the body's rhythm too often becomes disjointed. The head swings loosely forward, the shoulder girdle and shoulder blades fall away, and weight becomes unequally distributed. There is a falling away from the imaginary center line. At such a time, the total weights of the levers (arms, hands, and legs) are not assimilated in the complete pull or "rooting movement" through the pelvis to the bench, and in the complete suspension to the top of the head. There must always be a proper balance of all weights at the points of their spinal attachments.

Of all ages, perhaps the child understands and feels the truth of this principle most readily. Frequently, children at play make towers of building blocks, carefully placing the blocks with the weight concentrations directly over each other. This is a natural

At play, most children unconsciously center weight blocks directly over each other to achieve balance. However, the conscious learning process is so intricate that these same children cannot see any relationship between the principles they employed at play and those used in making music. (Photo courtesy West Point Pepperell, Carpet and Rug Division, Cabin Crafts Products, Dalton, Georgia.)

building process for them; they scarcely think about it. The difficult task is to ingrain this theory and experience of weight alignment in the pianist so that he, too, will distribute his weight accordingly. The difference between the material blocks that serve as the child's toy and the animate human blocks of weight lies in the fact that the live form is sensed through bones which are balanced in action.

The three blocks of body weight (head, rib case, and pelvis) are aligned in such a way that the balance of their combined weights is centered in the plumb-line gravity axis, that is, in the imaginary line extending from the head through the middle of the weight centers to the bench. The musician's plumb-line gravity axis should succeed in merging the "up" of life's energy and the natural "down" of the earth's gravitational pull. When it moves as a whole, the body always assumes the direction of the intended motion, and *the center line of balance is always ahead of the articulators; that is, the hands, arms, and legs.* As a basis for a fundamental technique and rhythm, every teacher should have a placard in his studio reading: "KEEP ALL WEIGHTS CENTERED IN THE SPINE. STAY WITH YOUR SPINE."

The utility and practicality of the structure of the human body is undeniable; and the pianist, if he uses his body to its fullest potential, will have the indispensable basis for a total performance. By centering weight and controlling the body structure, man may conserve both muscular and nervous energy. The pianist particularly cannot afford to scatter his energies by allowing his bony structure to become unhinged. If he does, he will tire quickly and his performance will be affected.

The balanced mass of the entire body gives direction to the parts or levers. An exuberant musician becomes so intense in his emotional drive and intellectual grasp of the myriad patterns that he pulls out, up, and away from, while pushing down into the sensitized, balanced center. The resultant bodily distortion is always in direct proportion to the intellectual-emotional drive. Occasionally, the drive is misdirected, and it is then wrongly forced through the shoulders, neck, knees, arms, and collar bones as individual units rather than as factors contributing to and maintain-

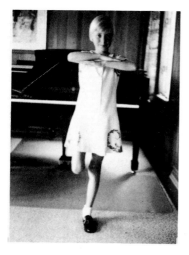 

These students are participating in a "pre-piano experience." They are demonstrating center balance and "readiness for action" in freeing their arms and legs.

The student is sensing movement which is initiated from the center of the body. She gives a quick "toss" through her spine, and her arms follow the line of her body. The center is always ahead of the articulating levers.

ing a focal balance through the balanced center. Again, the pianist's primary concern is to keep the weights centered and balanced in the spine.

A living balance is, quite simply, readiness for action. The images of such preparedness that immediately come to mind are the sparrow perched on a wire, or, more actively, the tiger preparing to leap. Our success in balancing our own bodies depends wholly on our knowledge of where and how our various weight blocks sit, hang, or are braced. This awareness, in turn, depends upon our kinesthetic sense. We either are "naturals" and can balance our bodies without help other than imagistic stimulation, or we require additional training and conceptual understanding.

The student imagines that she is crawling like a lion. She is strengthening her lower back and is developing coordination of her arms and legs through their deep association with the spine.

The closer the weights are drawn into a fine plumb line through the structural bony center, the more readily the body can carry a long-line flowing rhythm. Often, the futility experienced by the student is due to a lack of noticeable progress, which in turn is due to blocked movement resulting from the dissolution of the center line. Music teachers most frequently distort their own center lines because their patterns have been more deeply entrenched over a long period of trial and error.

The spine can be "lengthened"; that is, it is possible to maintain a long torso and to "lengthen" the spine by inner balance. All weights draw into the center line or spine to travel to the sit-bones (ischia) or pelvis. The bench is the prime resisting force and support, aided occasionally by the feet and legs.

How frequently a teacher of piano asks his student to "sit up straight" or "sit tall"! What the teacher does not usually realize, however, is that "sitting up straight" is not an action which is independent of the total body forces. The student must first sense a genuine base of support through the entire spine. This base must sufficiently support and initiate the motion which will carry the levers of articulation, that is, the arms, hands, and legs.

It is common scientific knowledge that *all energy generates through its pole and disperses horizontally*. The musician who has been trained to think, feel, and act according to this concept finds its application to the human body particularly meaningful. The ischia (sit-bones) can be sensed as being rooted into the chair, or as two electric prongs plugged into the current of the universe. The chair "pushes up" to meet them and they "pull down" to meet the chair. The hip joints, through the pelvis, should form a line of thrust into and through the sit-bones to the chair. One must not confuse the hip joints (the break of the leg joints) with the hip bones.

For effective pedal technique, the pianist (and organist) should be able to lift either leg in one piece from hip joint to toes. All weight flows back into the sit-bones, focuses at the point of resistance, and does not press against the thighs. The student should practice this sensation until he naturally does not "pull" or "dump" the weight of his torso forward. He should come forward from his hip joints to the piano, but should never, "spill out" his weight.

When considered from the viewpoint of the pianist, the total bony structure has a fourfold function. First, the skeletal structure effectively resists gravity at the point at which the sit-bones meet the chair. In this way, the bony structure is vital in conveying a feeling of support, balance, and integrity to the pianist. This stabilization through the balanced center helps to make the articulations accurate. In addition, because of the flexibility of the spinal column, the pianist is made free through the center balance because the tension is taken from his joints and muscles. As a student once said, "Let the 'roots' rest in the chair."

The weight of the legs should flow back into the sit-bones, and should focus at the point of resistance.

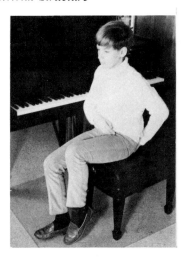

This student is showing the focus of thrust traveling through the hip joints, pelvis, and sit-bones to the chair.

The arms and legs are supported, connected, and suspended. Through hissing* slowly, they are drawn into the center line.

---

* See glossary.

Second, the bony structure furnishes the levers for the articulation of the musical idea and is responsible for the total rhythmic leverage.

Third, and perhaps most important, the spinal column is, for our purposes, the center of stimulus response for implementing all movement from center to edge.

Fourth, the spinal column is the place of attachment for the diaphragmatic (breathing) center, which in turn generates energy, the substance of rhythmic motion and the fuel for all dynamics.

Essential to the successful, total performance of the pianist is a rudimentary understanding of gravitation. The human body, like every other earthly entity, is subject to the downward pull of gravity. Gravitation is, of course, necessary to the pianist for support and power. The pianist must figuratively pull into a crouch as an animal does (collecting the potential for movement in the rear lower parts of the body) so that the center of gravity may be lowered and a base of support for freeing articulations established.

Man consciously controls his bones in response to a neuromuscular stimulus. Because we can command our bony structure (although certainly not the nerves and muscles surrounding those bones), we can and do think of the bones as serving supportive functions for our skill patterns. Of course, bones also serve as levers. The skeletal structure is instrumental in implementing the musician's desire to send a musical thought in space-time "from here to there." The musical idea is first conceived within its totality, and the center line must be a vital part of it. The arms, hands, and legs in defining the musical content must follow through in the moving stream of wholeness if the musician is to be successful in clearly transferring the patterns involved.

The pianist must sense the two bones which constitute the base of the ischia as one center base. They serve as "rocker bones," and enable the pianist to come forward to the keyboard without distorting the energy balance within. The pianist's overall feeling should be one of balanced security. If the pianist is balanced correctly, the four legs of the bench will receive equal shares of his weight. The performer does not roll around on his flesh when the sit-bones are balanced, focused, and rooted with the pull of gravity. The resistance offered by the bench to the pianist's "rooting" movements allows for expansive movement.

One has only to observe a great artist to note how carefully he attunes himself to this fine balance. Vladimir Horowitz is the perfect example of an artist with an exceptional inner balance. The balanced body can be likened to floating architecture; it is both alive and dynamic.

HEAD

We have stressed from the beginning the importance of a dynamic but composed center line which stretches from the top of the head to the chair. If a center composition is so important,

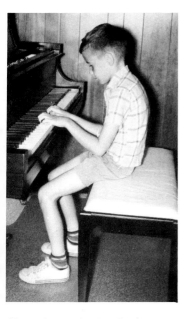 

Here the student's playing mechanism is receiving little support. He is not balanced and his arms are "dead" weights.

Here the student is balanced, supported, and connected from his sit-bone base to the top of his head.

one may justifiably question why certain artists practically allow their heads to rest on the keys in moments of intensity and during extremely difficult passages. It would appear to the untutored observer that in bending to the piano, the artist has lost all awareness of the balance within.

If such an artist is truly gifted in sensing musical output, bodily distortions will not disintegrate the "carrying-line" from within. If the performer sufficiently balances with the pull of gravity, suspends and supports his body weights through the spine, and can still manage the touches and release of energy in key timing, there is no reason why one who is so obviously gifted cannot bend and twist as he pleases. No concept, after all, should be so rigid that it may not admit of exceptions. Such a pianist is simply expending more energy than he needs to, and his playing probably will not be as substantive as it otherwise might be. Certainly, no less gifted performer should attempt such movements.

Individuals who are more concerned with seeing a performance than with hearing it are usually offended by the gyrations of such an artist. They usually declare audibly to the person sitting next to them that they really "cannot bear" watching Mr. So-and-So play. Generally, these people unconsciously sense that the finest performers are those who keep their center lines intact from the head through to the bench.

For the pianist who studies under the approach outlined in this book, a built-in remedy for distortions of the upper segments of the center line has become a part of the subconscious. This performer will understand, image, and practice keeping the weights centered in the spine. He is supported, as we have mentioned, from the top of his head through to the bench. He allows the natural pull of gravity to work for him rather than letting it work against his composure and center lightness. His head, then, is free in its cradle at the top of his spine. The support for the head is perfectly centered under the bulk of its weight.

The pianist who has no difficulty in channeling his "feeling" through the center living core of the bony structure, through the breath and energy, and through the music appears both poised and composed. He is a pleasure to watch. The audience participates in the musical experience with him and can relax and absorb the music. Victor Borge, for example, is a truly integrated musician whose incidental clowning and fun do not affect his center-line balance or performance.

Conveying the idea of the head resting free in the "cradle" at the top of the spine is not extremely difficult. The teacher need only mention a long-stemmed flower, such as a rose, which is rooted in the ground and sustained through its narrow center. Its head or bloom sits erect and regal atop its living structure. This image reminds the student of the dynamic creative stillness within his own center and helps him to sense the total inner balance.

One cannot easily effect a flexible head and neck structure.

This child is "spinning in orbit." He is developing a fine line through his center by narrowing his shoulder blades. His head is centered in the long line, and he is sensing both support and the inner "downward" mechanical force.

The pianist's control of his head is dynamically creative only in the total creative motion. He must learn to control it through habit rather than by a superficial gesture.

SHOULDER GIRDLE

The shoulder girdle is a bony, yokelike arrangement which hangs across the top of the rib case. It is not attached directly to the spine at any place. Its only bony connection to the body's skeletal structure is through the sternum (colloquially, the breastbone), which is connected to the spinal column by the ribs. The shoulder girdle is composed of the collarbones, sternum, and shoulder blades. It does not serve a supportive function in the body, but its very design enables the pianist's arms to move freely and powerfully in a wide range.

Some pianists both traditionally and erroneously refer to their shoulders as their source of power for their hands and arms. The performer's power, however, initiates from the ischia as they resist gravity at the point of contact with the bench. The power then flows from the center of the body, through the connection of the arms and sockets in the shoulder girdle, and into the hands. The shoulder girdle provides attachments for the many radially disposed muscles by which the arms are moved in all planes. The pianist should never allow his shoulder girdle to sink its weight upon the rib case, whether he is actively playing or at rest.

The body supports the shoulder girdle in two ways. The first is a suspensory sweep up into the head and neck. The second is a downward gravitational pull through the shoulder girdle, the ribs, and the spine to the weight base. The suspensory sweep up and the gravitational pull down through the center must be in perfect balance if the pianist is to be totally free in his movement. It often helps the student to maintain this balance if the teacher reminds him that the shoulder girdle is suspended from the head, and that at the same time two weights are hanging from the ends of his shoulder blades. When the shoulder girdle is perfectly balanced the outward tips of the shoulders hang directly over the median line of the ribs at each side.

It has been my experience that when this part of the body is balanced and supported from within for the first time, there are several noticeable and positive results. Many pianists who would never have played with any degree of freedom and satisfaction are finally able to free their playing mechanism. Their energy is unblocked and may flow unhindered from the center to the fingertips. The smile and light of discovery on the student's face is easily worth the long hours of research and the hours of mutual struggle.

When the student has freed his shoulder girdle for the first time, he is astonished at how "easy" it is to play and at how "right" he feels. The student who has always sensed his arms as a "side load" has finally relocated them in his lightly balanced center by the merging of the upward and downward forces, and he now feels a oneness of his body structure from his sit-bones to the top of his head. The teacher might justifiably draw up another placard

The weight of the arms should be transferred from the sides of the body to the center balance. The teacher is reinforcing the gravitational pull through the sit-bones to the chair.

for his studio which reads: "KEEP THE WEIGHT OF THE ARMS IN THE CENTER LINE."

The proper balance and positioning of the shoulder girdle is best conveyed to the student by having him feel the difference between proper balance and imbalance. To communicate the sensation, the teacher may place his hands under the student's armpits and lift the entire bulk of shoulder weight toward the head. At the same time that the teacher is doing this, the student should be narrowing his back by rotating his shoulder blades downward closer to his spine. While intent on giving the student the sensation that the whole shoulder girdle is balanced over the total body, the teacher should watch lest the student help him lift his weight. The student's insistence in this case results in his pulling out from the center line and in his tensing with the shoulder muscles.

A second participative exercise which is quite useful requires the student to flex his arms at the elbow toward his body. Reminding the student to keep his arms balanced near but not clamped to his body, the teacher proceeds to lift the entire shoulder girdle from the point of the flexed elbows. Through this exercise, the student learns to feel the arms and shoulder girdle as a unit. The arms and shoulder girdle are suspended and "float" in one piece, supported from below by a dynamic structure.

Should either of these two exercises fail to give kinesthetic awareness or to convince the student of the structural and functional unity of the arms and shoulder girdle, the teacher may turn to the bird-cage image discussed on page 38. The weight of the shoulder girdle must be assimilated into the center line before the student who grabs with the muscles of his forearm, top arm, and shoulders can be freed. This grabbing is the seat of the trouble.

RIB CASE

The rib case, in its relationship to the long-line axis of the spine, is an important area for the teacher to observe if his student is ever to play easily. If one unit along the spine is out of balance, counter-pulls occur along the axis to compensate for the weight which is off center. These counter-pulls effectively block any

Sensing the weight of the shoulder girdle and the top arms as though they were supported in two slings gives the student a kinesthetic experience of freeing and centering his weight.

The teacher is assisting the student in stabilizing and balancing the sternum and in centering the downward force to the chair by keeping the shoulder blades close to the center line.

energy which might flow from the spine to the levers. Blocked
energy interferes with the freedom of the levers attached to the
supporting structure.

The musician is a very frequent victim of rib case imbalance.
Unknowingly, through either emotional or physical disturbances,
he himself distorts the rib case balance by pulling his arms out of
the center line, by pulling on the sternum, or by attempting to
stabilize the body by locking the rib case. The problem arises when
the teacher discovers that any remedy is unlikely to aid the bad
alignment unless it is in some way associated with breathing and
proper breathing techniques. Suggestions for dealing with this
problem will be given in the chapter on breathing.

Often, bad rib case alignment can be prevented by using clear

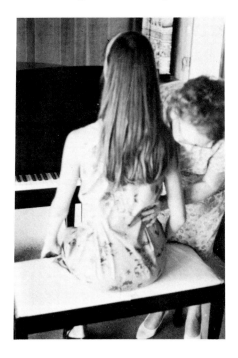

*The teacher is assisting the student in supporting her rib case and
in balancing it in the center line over the pelvis.*

imagistic concepts in discussions with the student. The teacher may ask the student to imagine the ribs as "ribbons" which, when hanging, suggest the shape of a lemon. When the student breathes easily and his body is well-balanced, there is great flexibility, and the breathing process is vertical like the movement of a pump handle. If a student breathes in and out high in his chest in a purely shallow manner, or horizontally like an accordion, he has not yet mastered the principle.

Another approach that is usually effective, especially with pet owners, is to draw a word picture for the student which says, in effect, that the individual ribs fold into the spine like the wings of a bird. It is also helpful if the student is asked to imagine a weight hanging on the end of each shoulder blade which pulls it down and out of the neck mass and into the area of the rib case. The rib case and pelvis must work together.

It is a common belief that students learn best by doing. To convey adequately the feeling of the rib case in alignment with the head, pelvis, and sit-bones, the teacher can lift the shoulder girdle and arms upward in support. The student then has the sensation of separating the weight in the shoulder area from that surrounding the rib case. He can be told to think of the weight of his rib case traveling down his body to the support of the chair. This exercise is valuable, for it allows the student to feel both the location and weight of the aligned rib case while remaining conscious of the total structure.

II. Practical Application

From the very first lesson, the teacher's goal should be to stimulate sensitive creativity in his student and, at the same time, to drill the necessary responses to the symbols. The student will become convinced through experiencing frequent contact with these concepts that music, which is born of equal measures of thinking and feeling, is carried totally into action through sound and motion. Both sound and motion are manifest in musical forms, which occupy and move through space-time. Sound is an embodiment of organized motion. Space-time is, therefore, the arena of the musician's activity; creativity and creative motion cannot be separated in reality. The first steps toward a creative technique are as applicable to "Mary Had a Little Lamb" as they are to *Sonata 109* by Beethoven.

The teacher may rely on some useful aids to help any student, regardless of age, understand this complex idea. Primarily, the teacher may call upon an intelligible system of imagery. In this case, images of wholeness (such as wheels, circles, and so forth) are most helpful because rhythm completes itself in ongoing spirals, and the student can easily relate the concept and the image that represents it. Second, the teacher may appeal to the child through his feeling for or sense of wholeness, that is, through kinesthesia. Third, the teacher and student may observe and discover their environment together. The student may be taught to see entirety rather than fragmentation. Fourth, and perhaps most important and valuable, the teacher may relate the principles that the student learns at his piano lesson to all of life. In this way, the musical aspect of a student's life is integrated with the rest of his experience. Music and the principles we are propounding do not become simply another unrelated fragment in an already fragmentary existence. As the body is drawn together through this approach to music, so the diverse elements of a student's life may be congealed by these natural and universal concepts.

Perhaps one of the most difficult ideas that a teacher must present to the student is the fact that together they are discovering music through playing the piano. The student, convinced in his early years of the semantic difference, at least, between players and instruments, is understandably taken aback when he is told that he himself is the real instrument. As he gradually gains confidence in his ability to explore and act through his own musical potential, he realizes that he is the individual who must understand and interpret the sound-motion relationships.

The discerning teacher may approach this problem of belief and conceptual readjustment by asking the student meaningful, leading questions. Besides allowing the student to arrive at his own conclusions, such conversations help remove any reserve and hesitation the child may feel. The teacher may challenge the child's mind early in their relationship when he asks the student when he "made" his first music. This question is frequently met with much vagueness in the child who is trying to answer in just the right way. A gifted child may point proudly to the fact that he has picked out several tunes on the piano even before he had lessons.

After commenting suitably on the child's reply, the teacher may call attention to the fact that the doctor wished him to cry immediately after birth. Often this observation elicits questioning looks, and the teacher may ask, "Do you have any idea why the doctor wanted you to cry?" Many children know that when they first cried, they began breathing. Acknowledging the correctness of this response, the teacher may observe that "To breathe is to be alive. Without life's breath, we can create nothing. And do you know," he might continue, "that from this beginning we have the seed of sound from which all music grows? Something within us wishes to be said, so it moves through our thinking and feeling. As it grows and matures, we have come to call it music."

Of course, such a step-by-step exposition is not necessary with many students. While stressing and awakening a response to music itself, however, the importance of exploring, understanding, and responding to the printed page as symbolic of sound and motion should not be neglected. The essential point to make with the beginning student is that through history, the great, creative musical masters have left us copies of their music with signs (pictures) of music printed on paper. The student will benefit when he understands that much of the challenge of music is being able to discern the thinking and feeling of these masters through sound and motion, and through the careful and respectful study of these symbols or musical pictures. Giving the student this information will help him to see why it is necessary for us to spend time recognizing the inner meaning and feeling of the legacy these masters have left to us.

All music is sound and motion. Anything else we learn is symbolic. The printed page, for example, must be sensed by the musician in sound-motion relationships, and as parts within the whole performance. The printed page, however, leaves much to be desired in the field of creative motion. Symbols in themselves can be misleading. The pianist or musician who plays "by ear" has bypassed the symbol as the first requirement. Such a student should not be discouraged; he should simply understand the nature of, and be guided into furthering, his intuitive gift. When he can no longer assimilate and imitate the content of the sound and motion, he must be able to interpret its symbols. Simply stated, the student who plays "by ear" must learn to read what he already hears.

The average student is usually very concerned, and understandably so, with symbols. Unless the teacher is able to keep his interest through the lure of sound and motion, the student's interest soon wanes. For the musical child, the drilling on symbols becomes quickly related to sound and motion; that is, the child learns that a note is a picture of a sound. Also, he learns from experience and repetition that a treble clef on a staff is indicative of a pitch ranging approximately from his "middle voice" to his "high voice." Furthermore, he recognizes that the time signature

2/4 defines a measure as space consisting of moving sounds.

In addition to this interpretation of symbols, however, the student's awareness of a space-time continuum must be awakened in which he counts "two" to create space. A half note fills the space of two. We move through the space of two; we *do not* hold a note "two counts." We *are not* referring to outer movement; we are awakening the feeling and control of inner movement. "Forte," "piano," and all dynamics should eventually be sensed in a gradation of energy from within.

Going to the piano, the teacher must make the point that the kind of music the student will create is directly dictated by the way he moves over the keys. The teacher may inform the student that by being observant and by watching all of life (people who are agile or especially skilled at their tasks), and by studying the laws of motion, he can learn many things that will help his thinking and feeling in playing the piano.

If a teacher can freely employ the terminology of the space age in his discussions with students, he will probably be more effective than if he persists in using the terminology of his own generation. The student thinks through these symbols in his environment, and his teacher's use of the same symbols will help him to assimilate material that would otherwise bore him. The teacher must enforce, for example, the idea that it is energy rather than weight which is vital in producing a "forte." To convey the idea that energy for dynamics and rhythm is organized and channeled from within, such clichés as "on the beam," "in the groove," "on the ball," "collect yourself," and "pull yourself together" are excellent. The student finds that he can more nearly translate what the music embodies. Certainly, such phrases are far more picturesque and precise than unnecessarily long and involved quasi-scientific explanations that both confuse and bore. Of course, many of the previously mentioned expressions were common currency long before the 1957 Russian orbital flight of Sputnik, but the point is that regardless of the date of the expressions, children react and relate to them. Often, the teacher can express an idea far better through the use of such clichés than by using his own words.

Preparatory to the serious parts or to the specifics of the lesson, the student should be made aware of a whole "collected" body. Awareness of wholeness may be renewed frequently by imagery. The teacher says, "Sit on your sit-bone roots. Let the chair hold you," or "Imagine, Johnny, that you have a tiny pole like a flagpole through the center of you from your sit-bones to the very top of your head." The student who tends to be especially disjointed in the way he functions is asked, "Let your legs float up from the hip joints, and let the weight of your legs drop back into the chair. Feel your legs in one piece." The child who persists in seeing small parts rather than the whole can best be assisted by swinging in an "orbit" from his sit-bones to the top of his head. He can be told that he should "feel in his own orbit." The piano student's whole world should spin from his two sit-bones.

There are three proven images that are usually successful in conveying to the student, in terms he can *feel,* the concepts that have been the subject of our first chapter. First, the teacher asks the student to imagine that he is a roly-poly doll with a weighted base. As the doll responds to the dynamics of the push and recovers to a balanced center, so the child in imitation, with his arms folded in front of him, is to swing from a toss from the teacher and respond only from the sit-bone base. He should remain sharply balanced and rooted in the chair. The point to remember is that there must be no resistance anywhere except in the sit-bones which are resting against the chair.

In the second exercise, the child pretends he is a spinning top, an appealing image that is common to the experience of most children. A quick toss from the sit-bones is given from the center against the base. The top, after spinning awhile, gradually slows down. The child should be able to maintain an integrated center regardless of speed. This is excellent kinesthesia for keeping undisturbed forces at the center and is applicable to tempo changes later on.

In the third participative exercise, the teacher gently takes hold of the top of the student's head and declares, "Imagine you are a bird cage swinging freely from a hook on a high pedestal."

 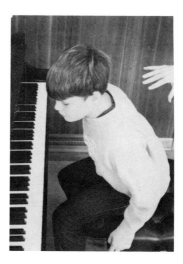

The student responds to the dynamics of the push and recovers to a balanced center. It is as necessary for the pianist to develop sensitivity to a finely balanced center as it is for the ballet dancer.

This student is performing a stunt which "loops" his arms into orbit.

This student is imitating the suspensory character of a hanging bird cage. He is feeling suspended from the top of his head. At the same time, he is giving a thrust through his hip joints and sit-bones to the chair.

This exercise strengthens the student's concept of suspension, while the other exercises tend to stress inner polarity and circularity with the sit-bones at the base.

Obviously, the imagery possible for use in such exercises is inexhaustible. Often, the child himself can contribute appropriate images. Such exercises stress teacher-student interplay in relating and sensing wholeness through the center.

Many eminent artist-teachers are vitally interested in balancing and in exercises that will promote better balance in their pupils. At a seminar at Northern Illinois University, the violinist Suzuki had his students lift their right leg, balance themselves on their left, and play. As an Easterner, Suzuki is representative of the Oriental interest in and awareness of inner balance and movement. We in the Western World have not been so deeply concerned with these, but we are quickly becoming alerted to the need for unifying the inner and outer.

For the pianist, the spine is the axis of all movement. The radius of the pianist's body patterns is not as large as in sports requiring expansive movements, but he must still exert a very precise control because his patterns are so small. The balance that the pianist ideally has in his spine is both living and vitalized. The motion that originates within the body through the spine is channeled through the levers to the keyboard. Athletes call this complete action the "follow-through." For every rhythmic cycle there is a follow-through.

Many piano students come to the studio with exaggerated curves in their lower and middle backs; they are, in effect, "swaybacked." It is impossible for these people to practice for long periods of time because they tire rapidly. In addition, such students are unable to produce the sounds they wish to hear because the power which originates "in center" cannot travel freely to the arms to support them as they move up and down the keyboard.

Some students can begin to correct this weakness by crawling on all fours slowly on the floor. The student must stretch his arms and legs as far as possible to strengthen his back muscles.

Often, too, in their attempts to balance their "life" forces through their centers, students are inclined to rigidity through the head, shoulders, and neck. When a student's body is in this condition, the teacher might ask him to collapse his center line completely and to breathe very deeply, filling his lower back with oxygen. Until students know how to use their lower backs as support for the arms while playing, they will continue to have this problem. I have called this exercise the "Dead Duck" because most students can picture a duck hanging from a hunter's catch.

One of the most effective follow-through techniques for use with children is called "How Do You Do, Piano?" This is a gesture symbolic of a greeting which consists of a follow-through from the hip joint break in the leg and torso. The idea is to keep the line connected from the head to the sit-bones as the child

The condition of a "sway back" interferes with the flow of power, rhythm, tone quality, and endurance. This condition can be corrected by focusing the energy through the lower back and pelvis to the chair and by gently stabilizing the upsweep through the sternum.

This student is performing the "dead duck" exercise, which is very helpful in freeing a rigid back and building support. She is filling her lower back with a deep yawn. As she resumes the balanced sitting position, she will sense her arms resting on foam rubber cushions. *(See page 41)*

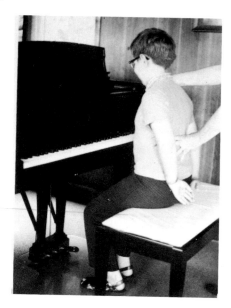

This student is performing the exercise, "How do you do, piano?"
His body is leading, and his arms are following in its path.

bends toward the keyboard. To further the student's awareness
of letting the body line lead, the teacher can place the child's folded
arms against his back so that they cannot possibly lead before the
power center.

A second exercise demonstrates that the spine is the axis for
all motion. The student allows his body to turn in one piece from
his hip joints to the top of his head. First the movement is to the
right, then back through the center, and then to the left. The arms
are allowed to follow only after the collected center initiates their
movement.

The collected center aids in retaining balance during lever
crossings. Weights must never "spill out" of this line, which implies
the pianist's kinesthetic awareness of his "opposite side" as he
turns. For example, if the pianist is turning to the right, he may
consciously need to "pull down" on the left side, and vice versa.

The teacher may ask the student to observe any one of the indisputably great artists to see this idea at work. After some instruction and experience, the student will usually be able to see that outstanding performers use this rotational movement although they may never consciously think about it. If the student builds these habits early in his playing experience, there is a good chance that they will become natural for him, too.

The final exercise that I shall discuss appeals to a child's love for action at any time and in any place. The teacher asks that the student put his left foot back near the center of the gravity line within the torso. Requesting that the child stand up quickly,

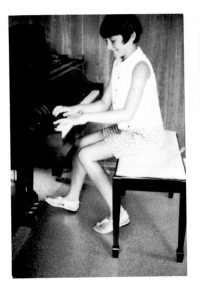 

In these photographs, the spine leads and the arms follow to the extremities of the piano. The student has a sensation of "through, up, and over."

This student's body is well-balanced as his hands travel up and down the keyboard.

This student is receiving additional support through the center from her teacher. The pianist's left leg is acting as a counterbalance.

the teacher notes whether or not the student breaks the line of his body in rising. This concept of rising on an unbroken line is an extremely difficult one for a new student to master. Many students come to the teacher very "dead," heavy, and broken in line, and it is an unusually arduous task to unify the concept and response. Needless to say, the teacher must be both patient and understanding.

It is vital for both teacher and student to notice that the artist's leg shifts nearer the invisible center line of gravity for balance and power. Eventually both will become sensitive to the distribution of the energy through the whole body. One who does have a sense of this distribution does not go to a concert and say,

This student is rising on an unbroken line of energy through the body. She springs quickly from the sit-bones (ischia) while maintaining her center balance.

"Oh, dear! I didn't sit where I could see his hands." The person sensitive to this concept who enjoys seeing and hearing an artist perform will be just as interested in the entire scope of the artist's performance as he is in the artist's hands.

The critical lesson to be learned from the application of these principles is that nature's laws for body control and motion become subconscious reactions in the whole act of playing. All feeling is eventually rendered into music. To have the student begin with no concept of a center of balance or feeling in his musical awareness, and with the arms, hands, and fingers leading the way, is to start the student on the road to discouragement. The student, when instructed in this manner, abruptly reaches the end of his potential and does not know why. Music stores claim that the bulk of their piano music business is suited to the first three years of study, after which time, evidently, the interests of most students turn to other things. This is extremely unfortunate for the student, for his hopeful parents, and for the teacher.

The second vital point to be learned from this lesson is that the teaching imagery for these principles, most of which are derived from nature, is virtually endless. The average child rejoices in such analogies and responds quickly and totally to such word pictures as a flower opening up from its center and the chick breaking its shell. The image of the tree is especially effective and useful for our purposes, for the trunk roots itself into the pull of gravity while it supports its branches and twigs. The average child has no difficulty in thinking of his torso as the trunk of a tree supplied with sap or energy to feed the whole living entity. For the child, his arms become branches, and his twigs and leaves (hands and fingers) are left to "flutter" in the wind, or, actually, in free facility patterns.

It is necessary to observe here that the entire lesson is not spent in teaching and in doing the previously mentioned imagery "stunts." Rather, the stunts are interspersed and balanced with other learning processes important to the piano. They are rehearsed over a long period of time until finally no thought is given to them. The stunts or aids to the total playing experience become habitual, and as they do, the student finds himself discovering the

This very young student is becoming aware of power in center.

This pianist is demonstrating power in, and traveling through, her center.

This student is feeling totally suspended. The mood inherent in Debussy's "Engulfed Cathedral" required the girl to sense the life force in an upsweep in order to produce the opening chords. She is also aware that to gather energy to release the "up and over," she must allow the resisting "down force" to initiate the first movement.

more complicated patterns of music. The subconscious assumes the directive function of the conscious.

As one of my students has said, "My bones keep me from crumpling up." Carrying this idea further, another student once declared, "My bones give my body a shape to carry the music." While these analyses reflect a child's speech patterns, the principles remain the same for all musicians.

III. The Levers and Their Behavior

When the artist seems to be still, his active forces, both emotive and mechanical, are in balance, and his kinesthetic sense of relaxation in this fine center balance is a reality. His body balance and coordination do not result from cultivating the action of individual levers out of relation to the rest, but rather from a sensitivity to the entire body and to the beauty of the total musical intent. The critical point is that the levers and their functions are not merely lifeless attachments which are joined to the body. The levers have a vitality of their own which is derived from the dynamic center within. When rhythmic motion is completed in cycles, kinesthetic awareness of it is sensed through every joint and lever.

Many piano teachers have an inexhaustible supply of exercises which ideally help the student to develop a greater and more fluid facility. I would concur with these instructors in saying that the student needs these exercises; however, I believe that such drills are useless unless they are rooted in a total technique. One technical pattern is not a whole technique. There is a gap between these fragmented, external, drilled maneuvers and the pianist's need for a totally cooperative system of leverage.

The levers with which we are concerned are the top arm, forearm, hand, fingers, and legs. We have repeatedly stated that the ideal center may be attributed to a dynamic balance, support, and connection. All appendages or levers should be balanced through their deep association with and connection to the one fulcrum, the torso. Interdependence of leverage is indispensable because of the need for the entire arm to be supported and carried by the torso in a rhythm of wholeness. Through the stabilization of the torso (the "master lever"), the top arm, forearm, hand, and fingers, joined as one piece, are supported, directed, and freed for movement.

Suspension of the arms is possible because of the transference and absorption of their weight from a side load into a flexible but stabilized center support. When the connected, supported levers are carried in this dynamic condition, the mystery of "betweenness" or the spanning of space is solved. Whether the pianist is playing, resting, or going from one articulative skip to another, the carrying-line remains unbroken. Not only are we able to maintain and control an ongoing rhythmic progression, but also we can assimilate the numerous keyboard articulations in the moving circuit. In fact, the pianist can release the keys correctly only if his levers are in suspension. The entire arm from shoulder to fingers must be suspended, and this suspension will allow each sound to be carried as an entity in itself and still not disrupt the flowing line by its singularity. "Betweenness" is established regardless of the interpretative necessity of touches. The overtones are not cut off. The music releases, travels, and finishes in ordered motion.

The much-used term, "floating elbow," often superficially maintained, is now possible. As an outgrowth of the balanced-center condition, the levers, supported at the weight-bearing places, now unfold from their attachments and should be able to make adjustments effortlessly as they undulate, rotate, flex, repeat, and swing in leverage. We are not minimizing the suggestion, "Keep the elbow floating." What we do not endorse is blind belief. When levers operate in a balanced plane within the function of the whole body carrying a rhythmic cycle, the levers do float. Floating in suspension is further improved through breathing deeply, and the condition is renewed through the breath impulses, which serve both rhythm and dynamics. A musical genius has a feeling of floating appendages because his response to the musical content pours emotion, mentality, and facility into one stream. Few musicians are willing to practice until they achieve this sensation of wholeness in motion.

The pianist's need to adjust the positions of the arm is further reason for the necessity of an adequate center support. It is necessary that the shoulder, elbow, and wrist joints be free to function through their balanced places of attachment. In the struggle of learning and with no concepts with which to free themselves, students acquire habits of pulling up and pushing down with their muscles, thereby causing fixation and holding in these joints. In their eagerness to release a desired tone or to meet articulative requirements, they grab with the muscles, an action which restricts rather than frees them.

If the arms were simply suspended in a straight line during the playing process, it would be simpler to imagine an axis through the center of the connected arm. The pianist's top arm and forearm, working as a unit, operate in changing degrees of extension and flexion; therefore, the dynamic axis which is the result of the balance between the mechanical axis through the bones and the muscle's "line of pull" is the one with which we are concerned.

Katharine Wells has stated what we have experienced in teaching: "The mechanical axis of a bone is a straight line connecting the midpoint of the joint at one end of the bone with the midpoint of the joint at the other end."[1] As she continues, the pianist's problem is clarified: "The axis of the segment does not necessarily pass through the center of the bony lever; . . ."[2] To the extent that the student is not stabilized in his center, that his levers do not balance at their natural places of attachment, and that he "goes after" articulations outside the rhythmic flow, he induces an imbalance between the mechanical axis and the muscle's line of pull. He must be helped to maintain a dynamic axis so that it is not necessary for his muscles to grab.

The freed joints will then release the tone and move the articulations effortlessly. It is at that time that the words "let it happen" take on an almost magical significance and balanced suspension is finally experienced. The student is able not only to freely telescope one segment into another, eliminating the leak

_____
[1] Katharine F. Wells, *Kinesiology* (Philadelphia, W. B. Saunders Company, 1950), p. 308.
[2] *Ibid.*

This exercise is particularly valuable for the student who has difficulty suspending his top arm or in "following through" to the keyboard. The movement pictured here is, of course, exaggerated. The arms must not pull out of the center line.

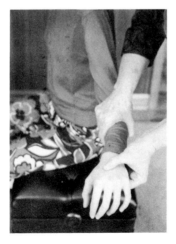

In telescoping the hand into the forearm, the student furnishes the forward "drive" while the teacher furnishes the resistance. The two forces are in action and are directed through a dynamic axis.

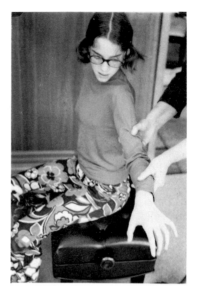

The teacher is helping the student to telescope her forearm into her top arm. The elbow joint is free, but there is no lost movement.

of energy, but also to proportion and move the levers in covering horizontal distance within the musical form. Many teachers are familiar with the contraction of small muscles but are at a loss to analyze the total line of action and to identify the "spot" that is blocking the energy.

Music itself establishes an invisible moving energy form. This form is initiated from the base of resistance and is completed in the playing phase. Motion that is sensed in wholeness in the on-going carrying-line assimilates the arm in the follow-through. Those who use the term "arm weight" cannot understand the validity of this concept. One does not think of "arm weight" when he throws a ball. Rather, he senses distance and timing and, giving a spring from his feet, he follows through. The arm, in this case, is simply an extension of the whole line of action.

In the total rhythm, the vertical release through the muscles surrounding the sit-bones and the diaphragmatic impulse initiate measured motion in a rhythmical unit. The levers fill the horizontal distance as they "pick up" vertical key-drops which are "tucked in" proportionately in the connected "in-between" suspended phase of the total rhythmic curvature. All creative motion is curved. Nature moves in curves as she stores energy, releases it, fulfills herself, and returns to create a new cycle. The performer adheres to this principle when his mind and feelings direct the dominant force from the base of resistance through the vertical torso and loop the horizontal placements on the keyboard in an unbroken cycle. Through vitally sensing the impulses and through directing and spending them in unbroken cycles, the pianist creates musical form. One simply cannot experience a total rhythmic progression in a detached vertical or horizontal operation. The vertical key-drop is not experienced as detached from the dominant rhythmical stream.

In creative motion, the levers perform as tiny curves within the great curvature. The greater always carries the lesser. As a great wave spins out tiny spurts, so the levers are spun out in one integrated curvature. As is evident in nature, even a raindrop does not fall in a straight line against the windowpane. The upward and downward forces curve in fulfilling the drop's destination. In observing the possible action of the individual levers, we notice that nature has provided a rotary component to complete the minute articulations which occur in the completion of the follow-through.

The word "elliptical" best portrays a picture of the shape in which energy travels through the body, over the keys, and then returns to base to complete a cycle. Its route through the vertical torso initiating the release of the dominant force should be focused very precisely, and this focus eliminates the temptation to travel widely, allowing the horizontal key-distance to distort the rhythmic form.

We cannot emphasize enough the importance of sensing the initiation of the impulse in a vertical direction from the lowest point of gravity. The placement and relative timing of each lever in the course of the progression are directly dependent upon the sensitivity of the accuracy and vitality of the stored energy released vertically and proportioned horizontally. Pianists tend to travel with "pitch" instead of following in the current of the rhythm. When the pitch lowers, they allow the center to disintegrate and the levers fall. Conversely, when the pitch rises, they "pull up" and race forward out of the rhythmic control or hold in their muscles. These tendencies to distort the physical action of the levers not only ruins the rhythmic flow but also seriously impairs tone quality.

Another tendency which influences the physical distortion of the function of the levers is to allow the eye to dictate the specifics of the performance according to the note progressions on the printed page. The performer is apt to yank, whack, chop, or reach ahead with the individual levers. He will not experience the joy of an encompassing rhythm.

Teachers often say, "Body before hands," in rightly perceiving that one cannot separate musical-rhythmical progression from suspended articulations. The rhythmic cycle always places the levers on the keys before the energy travels through the playing fingers. This does not mean that the key patterns are not covered by the hands before playing. Young students need to find the keys. It does mean, though, that an inner facility for sensing motion should be developed before the hands move an inch. This built-in awareness furthers the feeling of the rhythmic interrelationship between the detached vertical key-drops on a horizontal keyboard and the vertical push-off and follow-through within the body. Even the eccentric mannerisms of the artist are timed and occur in proportion within the commanding rhythmic form. If undue attention is given to the hand patterns and to hand position while the importance of a center control is minimized, then a disproportion of activity will exist between the levers and the body which initiates the dominant rhythmic progressions.

One must differentiate between a center support as the total fulcrum and what some pianists propound as a segment-fulcrum support; that is, the shoulder joint as a fulcrum for the top arm, the elbow joint as a fulcrum for the forearm, the wrist joint as a fulcrum for the hand, and the third knuckle joints as fulcrums for the fingers. Of course, the main action of articulative leverage is localized at the joints of any of the previously named levers, but an infinitesimal amount of vibration is felt through the entire connection of total leverage. The experience of a whole flowing power and total rhythm is disturbed if one conceives of levers in so many segments.

One should never shut off the sensation of reflexes through the whole line. Even in a tiny articulation such as a trill, where the localized action occurs at the knuckles of the fingers (the third joints), the sensation of the connection of the tiny undulation and rotating reflexes is still not shut off from the total arm. Also, the control of this tiny trickle of energy flow is initiated and controlled through the entire supported torso. Carrying a consecutive pattern as C–D–E–F–G with fingering 1–2–3–4–5 is not merely a vertical up-and-down action into the keys. The vertical and horizontal movement merges in an almost invisible spinning through a pinpoint focus through the axis of the forearm. Naturally, the vibratory action is sensed in the rotation-undulation function through the reflex joints. Even in a rapid repetitive action, the eye may register the pattern as vertical, but interacting forces (both vertical and horizontal) are active in an effortless performance.

It is helpful when the student learns to recognize the possibilities and limitations of his own set of levers. Individuals differ in their hand-finger spans, lengths of forearm, etc., and therefore, timing in the total rhythmic cycle will naturally be different for each person. To compensate for small hands, for example, faster and wider adjustments in the torso, top arm, and forearm will be required to cover horizontal distance. This should in no way upset the student's sense of the totality of the measured rhythmic progression indicated by the musical form. In finer and faster articulations, the relative speed and distance of the localized action have to be in proportion and balance within the total rhythm. In a totally supported, balanced, and connected system of leverage, the basis of support is ever the same. The slighter the performer, the more necessary it is for him to concentrate on the stabilization of the two forces through center to control the movements of the articulating levers. All of the adjustments necessary for skillful playing are served by the use of the force of gravity for the support and release of the creative life force.

Having sensed the total ongoing form, "dead ends" in the movement do not occur in the in-betweenness of adjustments. As the golfer learns which club to choose to travel a certain distance or height, so the pianist can develop his intuitive sense to release and control the levers which will articulate the desired curvature of the musical form.

One hears repeatedly at seminars, "What books do you use for developing skill to play octaves, trills, and so on?" One rarely encounters any questioner who would like to know how to execute these patterns skillfully and easily. Many would look askance if they were told that the levers are one with the body and that the torso is the one great fulcrum which supports and initiates the movement of the timed levers within a total rhythm.

TOP ARM

Far from functioning as some pianists believe it does (as the one source of power in the body), the top arm is actually the follow-through of the total playing process. Although the total arm is capable of a rotational adjustment, it does not initiate the basic rhythmic motion; rather, it serves as a conduit for the total rhythmic line. As the energy flows into the multiple leverage, the top arm working with the torso functions as a bridge between the torso and the more active playing levers such as the forearm, wrist, hand, and fingers. Its prime role is that of an associate stabilizer with the torso. Awareness of the top arm lever as an indispensable aid to the control of the articulations of the forearm, can be sensed if one turns it (top arm) simultaneously with the forearm and hands, (palms up) keeping the arms partially extended forward in one piece. Sense the suspended top arm resting in the base of support. Then merely turn the forearm bones and accompanying hand into the normal playing position. The freedom of forearm rotation can be enjoyed without disrupting the balance and control of the top arm. Students never cease to be amazed by the horizontal distances they are able to cover by an infinitesimally small turning in the top arm in cooperation with the forearm. After the young student is able to support his top arm from base, he can immediately be alerted to the fine adjustments through the top arm controlling the total playing apparatus and horizontal distance. In so doing, he will be spared years of fruitless practice and frustration.

Employing the top arm as a conduit for the rhythmic line can convey an important kinesthetic experience to the pianist. The following imagery for communicating this sensation of wholeness has been suggested. Imagine you were chosen to transfer a priceless, fragile bowl in a museum from one case to another. With slightly outstretched arms and hands telescoped into a stable body, you proceed. If you should push against the bowl, it will crush, and if you drop it, it will shatter. The top arm, in this case, serves as the bridge of stabilized control between the center (body) and the extremities of the fingertips.

Similarly, the pianist should allow his arms to draw into their sockets with no loss of energy. The arms are made secure in their sockets by a spiral wheel of muscular tissue. An increase in tonus enables the muscles to keep the weight stabilized by telescoping the top arm into a stabilized shoulder girdle and center support.

Teachers are properly alarmed by students who clamp their upper arms rigidly to the sides of their bodies. Their clamping is usually unintentional and results from lack of support through the center as well as from emotional insecurity.

The opposite extreme of clamping is demonstrated by the pianist who has no sense of inner attachment, a practice which results in a loose, floppy, purposeless arm movement. This condition is very likely to create keyboard inaccuracies. Also, gradations of intensity go begging for a direct channel through which energy can be carried.

In cases of a rigid or lifeless top arm, "the bird is hanging on the wing; the wing is not hanging on the bird." By starting at the base, drawing the "seat muscles" together, and rooting the sit-bones firmly into the chair, one can start a network of "drawing together" traveling up through the spine and into the arms, thereby giving a feeling of collected energy; the wing will again be "hanging on the bird." In a body so connected, the top arm is the major link between the base and the most active playing levers. A timely slogan is, "One carries two; two carry ten." Translated, we arrive at, "One torso carries two arms, and two arms carry ten fingers."

An indispensable function of the top arm in extending the rhythmic line is the control it provides in measuring keyboard space and in placing the levers. The follow-through of the more active levers is proportionately released and is further controlled by the extension of the top arm.

The teacher may best help the student correctly place and lighten the load of his top arm by lifting this section of the arm from the flexed elbow, and at the same time giving a thrust upward and inward into the arm socket. Simultaneously, she should give the student a thrust downward through the same shoulder. In time he will naturally feel the support of the arm through the center and the freely suspended arm. Also, the teacher can gently pull the student's arm sideways from his body. The student should resist slightly, just enough to feel connected and still not be holding or clamping.

The glissando is most helpful for conveying the idea of the unity of the top arm and body. The student establishes a resistance to the chair through his sit-bones, while his top arm remains vitally connected through the center structure. The continuity of the movement is maintained within the suspension by the blend of the two forces.

The patterns found in the compositions of Mozart and Haydn usually necessitate top arm suspension (suspension close to the spine). When pianists cannot support, connect, and suspend the weight of the top arm, these patterns are difficult to control. Because of their difficulty with suspension and support, some pianists perform the works of Mozart in a manner suitable for playing those of Rachmaninoff. The condition of the top arms (as well as the musical interpretations) of these pianists is not satisfactory.

The indispensable functions of the top arm are that it operates with the torso in stabilizing the many articulative movements of the most active levers, gives direction to keyboard distance and aids in the placement of levers. The top arm is controlled by the whole body in a balanced rhythm.

FOREARM

Kinesiologists inform us that a ". . . mechanical axis . . . is a straight line connecting the midpoint of the joint at one end of the bone with the midpoint of the joint at the other end."[3]

The pianist particularly needs to sense the interaction between the mechanical axis and the shortened muscles. A dynamic axis through the entire arm is realized when the connected, balanced bones are moved by the shortened muscles operating in the direction of the line of force.

Our goal in perfecting a skill is to eliminate superfluous movements and unnecessary tension as we move through the shortest circuit of the dynamic axis. The reciprocal systems of leverage, sub-fulcrums, ligaments, and tendons cooperate in reaching this goal if imagery and kinesthetic awareness are directed in the process of a continuous rhythm. The actions of the forearm are to be realized in relationship to this whole moving line. [4]

In considering the function of the forearm, one needs to be aware of the action of the elbow joint as a free-swinging hinge between the balanced top arm and the balanced forearm. Both levers can swing effortlessly when they are securely connected and supported through the center. The top-arm control never leaves the forearm stranded, forcing it to pull, fall out, or push ahead on its own. An innate sense of muscle pull, shortening, and lengthening through the dynamic axis as the arm adjusts over the keys places the levers adequately. Dr. Maier frequently called these horizontal spacings "skip-flips." In these "flips," however, the pianist need not think of contracting or of releasing his muscles. When balance and motion are established, muscles in their involuntary capacity move the bones.

3 Wells, *op. cit.,* p. 308.
4 For a more detailed discussion of this material, see Wells, *op. cit.*

In preparing for the extension of the arms to the keyboard, the shoulder girdle must be balanced through the two forces for ease of action. Crossings, skips, and meeting the demands of playing in the extremities are controlled in this manner. The shoulder blade sustained in the down force rotates and cooperates in the direction of the spine while the collar bone and sternum are gently stabilized in the up and forward sweep.

This student has a tendency to pull from the collar bone. These faults hinder the freedom of her arms and fingers. The teacher is testing the forward adjustment of the collar bone and is giving a downward thrust on the opposite side of the body.

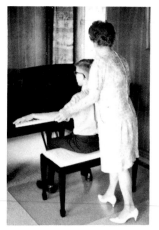

The teacher is helping the student support his top arm in a total rhythm. At the same time, she is testing the elbow joints for freedom of flexion in preparation for undulation, rotation, and repetitive action.

The student and teacher are testing the rotative movement within the arm. The rotation is carried in the forward progression of the rhythm. The tiny undulative component must not be restricted.

In establishing the balance of the two forces, with the aid of the teacher, the student is testing her freedom to make rapid repetitive movements of the forearm. The forearm has been freed at its place of attachment in relationship to the total arm.

The teacher assists the student in stabilizing the shoulder girdle and top arm as the student experiences an effortless flexion in making a skip-flip with the freed, balanced elbow joint.

Degrees of undulation: The rhythm has dictated the necessity of the "waves of undulation" *through the joints of articulation. This student has an unusually large hand span and it is not necessary for her to adjust as deeply. She is not reaching ahead with the small muscles but is allowing the axis of movement to direct the placement on the keys.*

An indispensable function of the forearm which is ultimately accountable for its being one of the most active mechanisms in the total dynamic axis is the twisting and untwisting of the radius and the ulna, one of which twists over the other. Such rotation as occurs in the forearm is an internal movement. Many pianists image only an outer forearm rotation, a limitation which causes them to render the fine adjustments awkwardly.

The function of shortening and lengthening leverage in adjusting over the keys can be visualized as an undulating (wavelike) cooperative process between levers. Actually, this undulating movement is interacting with a tiny rotation traveling through the dynamic axis, because *all* muscular activity has some rotary component. There are several pitfalls for the pianist who cannot "let go" and allow the movement to roll in waves through his joints, or for the pianist who goes to the other extreme of "flopping" too loosely in the undulation. These failings interfere with the total rhythm, leaving a disproportion between the center and the levers.

By helping the student with support and connection, the teacher can assist him in maintaining the integrity of the dynamic axis between the top arm and forearm. The teacher should place one hand under the student's top arm while the other hand supports his forearm. This movement helps remove the "grab" from the muscles surrounding the elbow joint, frees the wrist and fingers, and directs the energy to the keyboard.

WRIST AND HAND

Whether or not the acclaimed artist-virtuoso speaks to us emotionally, the fact remains that his music is spun out in space-time form which is imbedded in anatomical completion. His completed articulations* are infinitesimally and efficiently blended to become a part of the follow-through to the keyboard, which is closely associated with the quality of tone. The artist is utilizing the pull of gravity as a stabilizing base and focus from which to initiate a rhythm rather than going doggedly ahead grabbing segmented leverage in a digital progression.

---

* See glossary.

In speaking of possible articulations of the arm and hand, we are eager to clarify that no reference is made at this time to articulated motives, slurs, and so forth, for example, those occurring within a measure or line of Bach's music. The intuitive composer does not, however, insert harmonic, melodic, or any other idioms of musical units unrelated to the ongoing carrying-line. Musical progression which requires orderly proportion and exactness of articulative skill cannot be hindered by anatomical clumsiness. Artistically and rhythmically, the intended emphasis in the music occurs in the unfolding progression.

Because of the merged energy of the two forces channeled through the dynamic axis, the cooperative interaction of the top arm, forearm, hand, and fingers warrants giving attention to the wrist. The wrist is the last big joint through which the rhythm (energy form) passes before the hand and fingers complete the interacting articulations. *The wrist is never as strong or the fingers as free as when they are in close association with the top arm and forearm.* The function of this merger is best expressed by visualizing it as a pinpoint nucleus in the center of the wrist. Through this point of interaction, articulative movement is directed. The resultant balanced interaction is the reason for facility of flexion, extension, rotation, repetition, and cooperative undulations of the levers. *The greater levers initiate the movement and power, and the smaller units vibrate out of the total intention.*

Before the student becomes involved in pianistic patterns, it is wise to help him sense the two forces through his hands. The teacher might ask the student to close his hand as a boxer would and, at the same time, direct a thrust through the arm to the keyboard. This image is *not* intended to incite a feeling of "socking" the piano. At the same time, the teacher resists that thrust by directing the force through the shoulder socket and on down to the chair.

Even though the wrist joint is closely associated with the forearm, it is free to undulate, rotate, vibrate, and move from side to side horizontally. Simply to think "loose wrist" is a very devitalizing experience. The wrist is flexible and can adjust to rhythmic curvature and to the flexion and extension needed for covering keyboard placements. Because pianists tend to overreach out of

The student directs his energy through to the keyboard, while the teacher furnishes the resisting force to the chair.

The teacher is supporting the top arm and is giving the direction of force through the student's hand. This practice eliminates reaching with the small muscles of the fingers.

THE DIRECTIONS OF FORCE THROUGH THE HAND

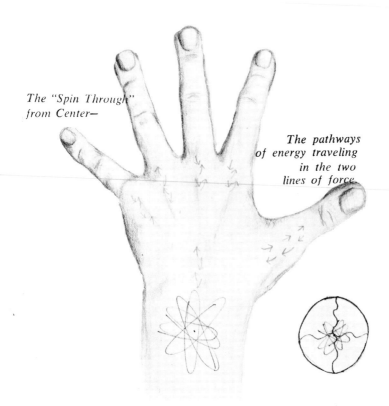

The "Spin Through" from Center—

The pathways of energy traveling in the two lines of force

The fingers can flex, swing, and rotate from the knuckle joints as they are spun out and are placed in the rhythmic curvature. A tiny spin originates from the sit-bones against the chair, follows through the spine and arm, and eventually focuses through the pinpoint in the wrist before traveling on into the finger tips. The center is ahead of the hands. Movement is not being "made" through individual segments unrelated to the whole.

the tiny nucleus of interaction and to lock the two bones in the forearm, there is frequently much strain at the wrist. When the two bones are locked, top-arm support and forearm rotation have been ignored. Also, the wrist joint suffers as a reaction to the cutting off of the undulative, repetitive reflexes generated through the whole dynamic axis.

In supporting the belief that all rhythmic progression is released from an inner kinesthetic experience of motion (breath impulses) and travels to the extremity of the fingers, we cannot assign piano playing to any set of "superimposed" hand positions. Such positions are only small parts in a fragmentary technique. The fact that energy cannot be transferred to the keys except through the contact of the fingers at the key level (by tripping the escapement of tone: hammer against string) is positive proof that the control of energy has to be channeled through the fingers. Notice, please, that we said *"through* the fingers." The disaster occurs when the fingers usurp the control of the power of the top arm, forearm, and even the hand. The small muscles take over by grabbing and holding; they remain unattached to the total suspension. This is still another reason for instilling in the student the control of the octave pattern; *a center control must be mastered before the student learns involved finger placements.*

Teachers who are concerned about turning a creative phrase and about student disinterest in the ordered vitality and placement of the individual note values within phrases very often have to resort to digital counting until the student can play in digital time. It is then that the fingers may assume complete control. As Artur Schnabel has said: "I don't believe in finger playing. The fingers are like the legs of a horse. If its body wouldn't move, there wouldn't be any progress; it would always remain on the same spot." [5] However, if constant attention is given to understanding and experiencing the concept of "the greater carrying the lesser" in controlled, impulsed units, as Schnabel indicates, musical shapes will, in time, appear, balancing the part within the whole.

A marked difference can be observed in proportionate lengths

---

[5] Artur Schnabel, *My Life and Music,* ed. Edward Cranshaw (New York, St. Martins Press, 1963), p. 137.

and widths of individual hand spans and finger levers. It is possible to regulate the flow of power through each finger as it flows through the center. In the ongoing curvature, each finger or combination of fingers falls into its placement in the arc of the moving cycle. Small hands are able to compensate in horizontal placements by flexing effortlessly through the joints more often and more quickly within a long rhythmic line. When the center suspension is secure, reams of patterns can be spun out which otherwise could not have been mastered by grabbing with the small muscles.

The hand opens from its base attachment to the forearm with a thrust through the extended first joint of the thumb (next to the palm) and a parallel thrust just below the knuckle joints between the fourth and fifth fingers. Actually, the drive feels just as if one had extended and arched his fingers forward out of the fist he made when imitating the boxer.

Another effective image for understanding and feeling the spread and power directed through the arch of the hand and fingers is to think of a lady at a glove counter in a department store being fitted for kid gloves. Her forearm and elbow are flexed on the counter, and each finger of the glove is drawn securely over her hand with the counter furnishing the necessary resistance. The lady is sensing the two forces merging through the direction of the axis. When she extends her arm, she does not lose this feeling of the total arch opening or of the connecting stream of power.

The vital principle which cannot be overemphasized is the degree of freedom in the flexion of the fingers. Flexion is influenced by the desired sounds, small forms, individual hands, and the need to be close to the axis of movement. Pianists who lift the fingers vertically while they are flexed vertically have without question cut off the rotary component. This blocked energy imposes restrictions on the performer, not only rhythmically but also artistically. When the rotary component is blocked and the young student loses the feeling of the encompassing sweep, "he has had it." Swimming, baseball, and skating become much more appealing for him than the frustrating small movements associated with playing the piano.

Tradition has insisted that long fingers are the trademark of the majority of skilled pianists. Observations of virtuosi, however, alert us to the fact that a broad hand and shorter fingers, with the resulting closeness to the center axis, are in fact more adaptable to velocity, control, flexibility, and melodic continuity. But be that as it may, we notice that an artist-virtuoso organizes his energies from within and balances the two forces through to the periphery of his hands, thereby compensating for any lack of physical proportion.

Imagery which may cause one to sense the hands as functioning in a total movement within one's own orbit is that of an aerialist ascending a rope ladder. The arches of the feet, the arch of the seat, and the arches of the hands are sensed as connected and alive to all extremities. The aerialist's feet give an elastic push which releases energy through the spine as he places his hands on each successive rope in a chain reaction.

It is imperative that the thumb swing freely from the first joint; it flips, rotates, and extends in one piece. When in balance through the center of the arched hand, the thumb cooperates as another finger. The thumb must never be the source of ugly, heavy bumps. It acts as a lever within the pinpoint axis of the undulating, free-swinging, rotational wrist. Children enjoy the thumb swinging from the first joint as a "drumstick" or chicken leg.

No pianist really senses a coordinated rhythm unless he senses a suspended key release. It is the supported release through the center which alows for the maintenance of the suspension of the continuous rhythmic line. *The fingers are merely finishing the rhythm which was initiated in the center of the body.* Every time the pianist drops a lever or loses the inner tonal balance through his fingers, he produces unpleasant sounds. The more he is able to clarify musical imagery, the nearer he will move to sensing the balanced relationship between the whole and the part.

LEGS

In the performance of the great artist, the legs are attuned to the torso, arms, and head in the total line of balance. Within a sensitive body which continually responds to the invisible musical content, the legs are not inactive and heavy.

The strength and cooperation of the legs with the rest of the body depend upon their closeness of association with the spine. Suspension is maintained from the leg sockets to the arches of the feet and toes, which remain ready to serve as articulators of balance and pedal technique. The legs make adjustments which ultimately affect power, balance, and dynamics. Control of the legs is as important to the pianist as it is to the athlete.

When the pianist senses rhythmic impulses in initiating phrase or measure motion, wholeness is felt in a connection through the arches of the feet, sit-bones, and hands. The line of intention dictates action, just as the lines of a cat's body indicate that he is ready to spring, or as the body lines of the basketball player show that he is poised to shoot for a basket. Creativity is served in sensing "from here to there" in space-time. The more organized the movement, the more certain the result.

In sustaining a long-line rhythm, a powerful passage, or both, it is necessary for the left leg to swing backward nearer the lifting line. This movement is usually most obvious in the case of sudden dynamics. Depending upon the intensity of the passage, the artist may spring totally from the bench. In the control of his body movements, he senses the two forces working within him. The lesser artist or student is apt to be "carried away" by these large patterns of body movement. He ignores the gravitational pull of the earth and crashes into the keys with an unpleasant percussive sound. As the late Dr. Guy Maier said, "Take the 'cuss' out of percussion."

When the pianist plays near the extremities of the keyboard, the legs help to stabilize the long line of the torso by balancing its turn through center from the sit-bone base. In this case, the leg stance naturally widens to help counterbalance the center. By compensating for the greater exterior movement in this way, pulling and bending are avoided and the arms are stabilized even further.

The would-be pianist must leave no leaf unturned in exploring the vibratory possibilities which the pedal can create in the tone-color palette. Through the demands of the musician's ear and his sensitivity to the motion within melodic and harmonic progressions, the pianist's legs, feet, and toes cannot help but be involved in the mechanics of articulating the three pedals. When and where the pedals are used to create the myriad effects which the artist of tone is ever exploring is entirely beyond the scope of this thesis. One knows only that when the pianist reaches any degree of satisfaction, certain conditions are in evidence. Pedal training should begin in the first lessons, for the lightweight legs are an integral part of the lightweight body.

The pianist can easily agree with Anton Rubinstein, who, in speaking of the role of the pedal, is alleged to have said that it can be "the soul of the piano." Who, for example, can play Debussy's *Clair de Lune* with no experience of suspension in the legs while pedaling? Debussy uses no "roots" in the harmonies for several measures. These inversions are cause to feel within oneself, from the toes through the top of the head, the rising of the moon.

The legs and feet are of undeniable importance to the pianist and to all musicians in general. Singers declare that they produce their tone from their legs and feet. The late Leopold Auer, the famous violinist and teacher, insisted that his students be able to lift either heel from the floor at any time and to pivot through the center of the body. One has only to notice the dynamic response through the feet and legs of the sensitive conductor to sense his response to the wholeness of the rhythmic form.

To give students the physical sensation of the role that their legs play in their piano performance, ask the student to sit back on his sit-bones as far as he can without sitting on the end of his spine. The student then places his hands on his hip joints, which should be directly centered over the line of thrust through the sit-bones and into the chair. Requesting that the student lift his legs alternately like a jackknife, have him "hiss" (refer to the chapter on breathing and to the previous illustration), allowing his spine to "lengthen" and his ribs to fold closely to the spine. He should not be allowed to push anywhere against his back or to let his weight spill out. This exercise will help to correct a fault which is common to many pianists, that is, pushing against and pulling from the lower back, a habit which ultimately blocks the flow of power through the center.

These techniques for developing the sense of wholeness can best be introduced through imagery, observation, and experience. They are assimilated so gradually that the child does not view them as extraneous to his total experience. In this case, it is helpful to ask a child to imagine that an elf is touching his knees with a wand. The elf's touch causes the entire leg to float effortlessly upward in one piece. From this beginning, it is a relatively easy matter to "float over" and to contact the pedals.

Until a child's legs are long enough to reach the floor without pulling out of the leg sockets and disturbing the whole balance, he should be given a footstool for support. If the footstool causes the legs to be too high in relationship to the torso, books should be placed on the bench so that the arms are balanced over the keys.

IV. The Fibrous Tissues: Connectives in the Total Performance

MUSCLES

It is not necessary to do an in-depth study of muscles to be a fine pianist. If one is a fine pianist, however, it is necessary that his neuromuscular system be operating sensitively and excellently. Muscles do need to be exercised and used, furnishing a very valid reason for the musician's continual practice. In a musical learning or performing experience, the mind images, the feelings anticipate and the nerve-muscle unit moves the articulators *automatically.*

Mabel Elsworth Todd has stated in *The Hidden You: What You Are and What to Do about It* that "Muscles are the power arms acting on the bones as levers. In organized movement, muscles must move bones away from centers (center) of support and back to center again."[1] This statement alone underscores our need to be balanced at the weight-bearing places so that the levers can move effortlessly in a total rhythm. Continuing, she says,

> Through reciprocal muscle-action this is accomplished. As each bone moves in relation to each other bone, the mean of the distance they move in opposing each other forms an axis. The direction they take is in line with this axis.[2]

For those of us who are not physiologists or physicists, these words may convey no kinesthetic relationship to the playing process. Imagine the caterpillar inching down the sidewalk. His direc-

---

[1] Mabel Elsworth Todd, *The Hidden You* (New York, 1953), p. 58.
[2] *Ibid.*

tion is in line with his axis. The movement of the "up curve" within his body opposes the "down curve," and vice versa. The median line of the power through the curves is the dynamic axis, and the distance he moves away from the median line formed by the curves determines his speed of movement.

We can transfer this concept to the action of muscles acting upon bones through a dynamic axis. In actuality, the axis within the center of the undulating wave through a pianist's arm dictates the direction of its movement. Conversely, our direction through the axis to the keyboard affects the curvature through the joints and the distance in and out. If the tempo becomes faster, the curves of the waves through the joints become shallower. To the pianist, this means that the faster the tempo, the less lost motion can be allowed. If the tempo becomes slower, there are fewer articulate waves and the troughs are deeper and the crests higher. Muscles are important to this consideration because they work reciprocally with the bony structure through contraction and release within the one continuous rhythm.

As motion and dynamics are anticipated, changes in respiration aid the muscle by supplying the necessary energy. The great muscle, the diaphragm, is the most sensitive one within the body. Every thought and feeling consciously or unconsciously affects our breathing and, therefore, the diaphragm. The genius usually needs no prompting concerning his breathing. The less gifted can improve through understanding this principle and can train to release and revitalize through the use of the "great breathing muscle."

An indispensable component of creativity is the ability to sense accurately filling space "from here to there." The pianist needs to become skilled in sensing through contraction and release the degree to which the nerve-muscle mechanism can fulfill the emotional expectancy of the music. The demands of the music cannot be met, however, by thinking about the names and attachments of muscles. Rather, fulfillment will automatically result when musical units are sensed creatively in space-time and the neuro-muscular system serves to move bones in response to motion and sound.

CONNECTIVE TISSUES IN BALLISTIC MOVEMENT*

. . . movement is initiated by muscular contraction, but . . . muscles then relax and permit momentum to complete the movement. . . . On a smaller scale it is represented by typewriting and piano playing.

When these activities are performed nonballistically, that is, with constant muscular contraction, they are uneconomical, hence not skillful. They are then tension movements. This characterizes the way beginners and young children frequently attempt new coordinations, especially when they are concentrating on accuracy of aim rather than on ease of motion.[3]

The pulling of the antagonistic muscles, the weak support through center, and the imbalance of the two forces are responsible for this poor hand posture.

---

* See glossary.
[3] Wells, *op. cit.*, p. 46.

The fingers are working ballistically. They are supported through
center, and are not pulling with the small muscles.

From a state of readiness, which necessitates sensing the hand patterns to fill the horizontal space on the keyboard, multiple articulations are kept intact. There is a constant readiness to proceed ballistically through the connection and conditioning of the connective tissue groups. As prevalent as it is for pianists to "grab" with the small muscles, it is equally typical of them to "let go" lifelessly in the fingers—or, for that matter, all through the body. Nearly everyone has experienced placing his finger in a tiny infant's hand and feeling the drawing together of the child's fingers. This imagery often works with students in helping them to sense just the right amount of "preparation" to carry the fingers the rest of the way ballistically.

The artist is able to "tuck" the intricate patterns into the framework of the total momentum both through his clear imagery of the patterns and through his use of the connective tissues. This response is instinctive, very much like the cat crouching ready to spring, and the skater or dancer completely connected from head to toes.

Almost every beginner of any age does some amount of "holding" with the antagonistic muscles in the arms and fingers. If the teacher stresses accuracy, desired dynamics, and velocity before balanced support and suspension of the small levers with the aid of the connective tissue groups, the student will never realize the freedom and exhilaration of a totally free rhythmic progression. This "holding" is a common bugbear for teachers, who most often face it when they accept a transfer student who has been allowed to play for a long time with tension in the small muscles. Such a student has never experienced the lightweight connective groups working in his favor.

A much-used pattern which the pianist meets daily and which is not always the easiest one to teach is the familiar waltz bass.

In maintaining a rhythm rather than a note progression, space-time distance is sensed before *C* and through the last chord. Necessary shortening of the muscles which initiate the impulse that will carry the first, second, and third beats occurs through the center and through the arm. Instead of grabbing or devitalizing the connective tissues, the student should lightly maintain the position of the chord and the hand and arm movements in between. This movement will fulfill the horizontal space of the organized, sensed impulse, and is similar to the follow-through movement of the athlete after the ball leaves his hands.

Countless patterns in pentachord progressions have been written for young students, progressions in which it is necessary to feel two, three, or more sounds being carried by the momentum of the impulse through ballistic movement. If the student cannot master these progressions, he will never have "fun" playing the piano.

V. Movement in Music

KINESIOLOGY

The Random House Dictionary defines "kinesiology" as "the science dealing with the interrelationship of the physiological processes and anatomy of the human body with respect to movement." For the musician, kinesiology is an awakening awareness of the anticipation of the desired response to motion and sound and to the gradations of dynamics.

Although this dictionary definition is more than adequate for our purposes, it is true that practical terminology and imagery for this relatively new science are lacking, especially in our Western culture. As man continues to reach into outer space and to acquire terminology which is quickly assimilated into the spontaneous play of the youngest school child, why cannot the music teacher inherit or create a comparable set of symbols based on kinesthetic experience of natural processes which will reach the inner space of his student?

It would be a rare musician, indeed, who could become an authoritative kinesiologist; nevertheless, the musician is learning to use this science to unify his inner and outer worlds. The sensitive musician experiences wholeness in sensing the "oneness" of skeletal, respiratory, and neuromuscular responses within the one encompassing rhythm. His ultimate goal is, of course, to employ kinesiology as a learning and feeling tool to increase the total musical experience. Nothing should be as important to the musician as the music itself.

The vibrations of sound, motion, dynamics, and the body's movement when considered as a whole or in part are recorded

The student learns to sense kinesthetically in many different situations. She senses the gathering of the life force to pick up and sustain the book. She is aware of balance, support, and connection from her feet to the top of her head and to the ends of her fingers. The teacher helps her to discover a like experience in her ability to collect, release, and spend energy in producing a desired tonal effect.

and interpreted through the kinesthetic sense. Our response to these aspects of our environment is awakened through understanding, through imagery, and, most of all, through experience. With repeated exposure to the environmental conditions and with continued practice, our response becomes habitual and is stored in the subconscious. There is certainly justification for saying that man earns this awareness through faithful adherence to nature's laws.

The kinesthetic approach to respiratory movement is, of course, no surprise to the vocalist or to the wind instrumentalist. It is far more likely that the pianist or string player would be surprised

by the role of the breath (in a kinesthetic sense) as an indispen
sable rhythmic control.

Even though it may be necessary as a last resort to induce a
feeling for creative motion, outer movement such as swinging or
swaying or other equally superficial gestures can constitute only
a hollow, dry musical experience. The sensitive musician would
be tempted to inquire, "Does he really feel what he is attempting
to express?" Emphasis, as always, should be placed on an inner
dynamic response to the music, which, with the skill of kinesthetic
awareness, can scarely be ignored.

THE TWO FORCES

Through observation, and through the use of definite procedures
which can be duplicated under given circumstances, we have
discovered laws regarding the conditions which we should provide
for ourselves in order to conserve energies and direct them into
purposeful living.[1]

Mabel Elsworth Todd has confirmed our belief that if one
learns more about the opposition of forces which establishes balance in all things, he may prepare his own mental, emotional, and
physical loads with more intelligence. The successful, energetic
teacher of music may not see the immediate relevance of this
statement to solving problems within his studio, but we make no
apology for such findings, and we find them readily applicable
to the piano and to all types of musical performance.

One of these principles concerns force. In engineering parlance,
the compression force traveling downward through the bones
transfers the body's weight to the ground or chair. The tensile
force operating vertically through the muscles attached to the
bones pulls the bones upward to the spine. The extent to which the
"up force" and "down force" balance each other determines our
feeling that "all is ready to go." With these forces in balance, the
pianist is relaxed and poised with a dynamic energy. The pianist's
total relaxation results from his fine balance.

The musician who would welcome a more factual approach

---

[1] Mabel Elsworth Todd, *op. cit.,* p. 92.

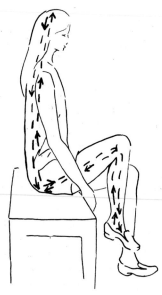

If energy is not blocked, the two forces travel the entire length of the body.

might prefer that this concept be cloaked in an aesthetic setting. As Eliel Saarinen tells us in *Search for Form: A Fundamental Approach to Art,* "A dry academic form of much knowledge and skill in handling the presentation, but lacking in the creative quality needed to make it breathe, is boring to the sensitive mind."[2]

Other pianists might welcome such terminology as: "rooted in the pull of the earth," or "lifted to the heights through creative vitality." Recently we observed a native Chinese teaching a class in movement in which he voiced this imagery: "Imagine you are moving to the bottom of the sea, but only to pick up a pin." He was stating how necessary it is that the two forces focus finely through the "one" center. If we are to be totally realistic, however, it is necessary that we accept nature's laws and rejoice in the kinesthetic experience of a point of rest within the freedom of sus-

---

[2] Saarinen, *op. cit.,* p. 280.

pension, a condition implied by these images. Because creative imagery is inexhaustible and is therefore individualistic, the search for creativity is exciting and satisfying. Even though intuition, instinct, and imagination are inherent in varying degrees within the person lured to music, creative imagery which sparks action for one person may be complete foolishness to another. The following image, for example, would probably be received in very different ways. The teacher might ask a student to imagine a lily pad floating in the water. The performer, as the lily pad, is sustained and lifted in a dynamic stillness by the two forces. There are lines of force moving downward through the water while the other force is moving upward with equal thrust. As the two forces converge, a perfect balance is created.

In balancing the body through the two forces, we have prepared the foundation for our emotions to be constructively channeled. Recently, in two different seminars, the students were repeatedly asked to "channel your emotion," and to "let the music flow." At that point they were given fragmentary, exterior pianistic technique and stylized suggestions such as, "In Chopin, one does thus-and-so." These are magnificent suggestions in musicianship, but if one's energy is blocked, how is he to release his facility to carry the music's meaning?

Once alerted to the truth that nature has only one system functioning through the body, why should the pianist be content with an outer, detached, unrelated procedure of "eye to key" which bypasses the substance of feeling? Stimulus of imagination and the desire to play are reasons enough for motion toward the goal. When feelings are sparked, breath is affected. Breath is the living substance which penetrates every cell in the body. When the child bursts forward with "See what I can play!" every cell in his body is inflated with the enthusiasm of life's "up" energy. Gertrude Murdough, a woman of great vision and a long-time teacher of piano in Chicago, found during her search for creative processes that students who breathed deeply maintained a total balanced line within the torso. As a result they were rooted in security at their bases and produced a very vital tone, regardless of their physique.

Last, but possibly most important, is the pianist's need for a quiet, dynamic center created by the balance of the life forces. If this balance is attained, then the physical struggle which crowds out musical intention will not be present. There is a story about Sabu, the East Indian child who lived in the forest. He said, "It is so quiet, I can hear the vibrations." Isn't this the essence from which music is made?

VI. Respiration as a Creative Means for Unifying the Rhythmic Performance

The Spirit of God hath made me, and the breath of the Almighty hath given me life.[1]

Man's imagination is a unique quality, a particularly significant element in his experience. It must have its roots in life, as do all his traits; and does not its splendor and luxuriance suggest that in man's living stuff there is a spontaneous quality that transcends simple mechanism?[2]

To merely exist is to breathe shallowly; to be healthy is to breathe fully; but to breathe creatively is to transcend the emotional and physical characteristics into the world of inspiration. In gratitude, we declare with the psalmist, "Let every thing that hath breath praise the Lord." [3]

The breath of life has provided the vitality for expressing emotion, whether through song or playing. The considerate performer adheres to the intention of the composer as nearly as he is able, but he unavoidably adds the life-quality of his own personality to the music.

It appears to the informed observer that many musicians could

---

[1] Job 33:4.

[2] Edmund W. Sinnott, *Matter, Mind and Man: The Biology of Human Nature* (New York, Atheneum Publishers, 1957), pp. 122-123.

[3] Psalm 150.

be freed emotionally and physically if they had been trained in breathing as the vocalist has. When the art of breathing is fluently serving the musical intention, breathing becomes entirely unconscious; for example, one can scarcely observe the breathing of a truly great singer.

We cannot honestly say, "Just breathe naturally," because breathing can be wrongly influenced by emotions and by both voluntary and involuntary body movements. Only when we understand, feel, and earn this natural condition which nature has designed are we free to play well. Conceptual thinking must contain factual thinking. Through imagination, factual thinking can take root in the reality of nature's endowment.

The virtuoso can be expected to execute intricate technical phenomena, but the artist-virtuoso has embodied the intensity of the music firmly within the "living stuff . . . that transcends simple mechanism." [4] Feeling has sparked the breath of life, and has permeated the performer's entire being.

One who is not so naturally gifted cannot turn on musical feeling, like running water in a fountain, by merely breathing deeply. However, many musicians are capable of releasing the feeling they do have if they learn, experience, and regularly use the breath as a creative tool in vitalizing, sustaining, and releasing a rhythm.

Fritz Kreisler has said, "Technique is mental." [5] I would agree. In Kreisler's case, music, mind, body, emotion, and breath were indivisible. When the musician "lights up" from within in response to emotive-musical stimuli, the response is supported by the breath of life functioning as nature intended.

DIAPHRAGM

To a degree, respiration can respond to voluntary directions. From observation, application, and admission of this simple truth,

---

[4] Sinnott, *op. cit.,* p. 123.

[5] Fritz Kreisler, quoted by Frederick William Schlieder, class notes.

the musician can afford to give attention to the intrinsic characteristics of the breathing process which are essential to the ease and
beauty of performance.

The most active and essential muscle in the breathing process
is the diaphragm:

> The diaphragm is a muscular and tendonous structure, of dome
> shape.   . . .   It is pistonlike in its action, bulging upward
> inside the cylindrical body-canal when it is relaxed in expiration,
> then downward when it contracts in inspiration.   . . .
> The diaphragm has no power to move sideways.   . . .
> The diaphragm must move down the spine to increase the
> depth of the chest cavity. In doing this it is joined by its lower
> accessory muscles, deep abdominal and pelvic muscles.[6]

It is apparent that all of these "accessory" muscles serve the
diaphragm and in turn are served by it in a balanced cooperation.

Low, deep breathing results in a low center of gravity. If
vertical depth is attained to the full extent of the stretch of the
thoracic (rib case) cavity, the expansion will accompany that of
the diaphragm. When the diaphragm contracts and lowers, the
ribs and sternum are lifted and the spine is lengthened by the
spinal muscles. The upper accessory muscles are often involved in
the process of respiration when overly expansive breathing does
not allow the diaphragm to complete its downward movement.[7]
"Hence, when you widen and lift your ribs in breathing you are
using upper superficial muscles, *not the diaphragm.*"[8]

Miss Todd cites the fighting animals and men who box or wrestle
as living examples of behavior which conforms to this principle.
If in the fight their chest and neck muscles pull up faster or harder
than the "stance" muscles pull down, the former interfere with the
diaphragm's excursion down the spine. In this event, the stance

---

[6] Mabel Elsworth Todd, *op. cit.,* pp. 113-114.

[7] Mabel Elsworth Todd, *The Thinking Body: A Study of the Balancing
Forces of Dynamic Man* (New York, 1937), pp. 217-244.

[8] Todd, *The Hidden You, op. cit.,* p. 114.

muscles cannot hold the center of gravity low, nor can the diaphragm supply the active muscles with enough oxygen. [9]

The intense concentration accompanying the playing of the piano is often attended by the tendency to pull upward in the chest, neck, and shoulder muscles before the diaphragm has had a chance to deepen. The support of the arms is markedly affected by the pull out of center. Because of this imbalance which inhibits the inflation and connection of the diaphragm with the associated muscles along the spine and within the pelvis, deep breathing is interrupted and strong trunk support is impaired. All such effects

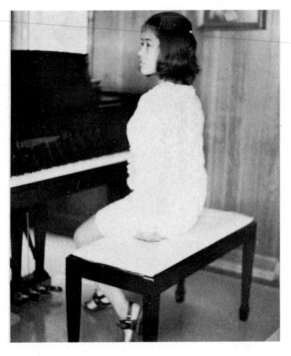

In performing the "quick yawn" exercise, the student is sensing inflation through the muscles of the sit-bones. Her sternum is floating, and the two forces are balanced.

---

[9] Todd, *The Thinking Body, op. cit.,* pp. 258-259.

are undesirable and are destructive to the stability, freedom, and suspension necessary to the pianist's ability to carry a long-line rhythm.

These difficulties can generally be averted by imagining and sensing an "axis of breath" through the cylindrical body canal. In keeping the symmetry of the rib case (the deepening of its cavity in relationship to breathing), the spaces between the ribs in the back must increase to equal the increase of the spaces between the ribs in front.

As ever, nature is consistent. If one is breathing correctly, cooperation between the functions of respiration, skeletal movements, and neuromuscular systems takes the same focus of direction to the earth's pull in preparation for releasing the upward and outward fulfillment of the rhythmic cycle. *In sensing a one-piece, balanced, lightweight body, we sense the breath as having filled all the cells of the body.* If this happens, the diaphragm has functioned to its fullest capacity.

EXPIRATION PHASE OF RESPIRATION

Almost every human being has stretched himself up and out in the breathing process, and has thereby partially lost his deep, central respiratory controls. By exaggeration and practice, we can reacquire the old unlearned breathing patterns in the harmonious action of bodily movements. Rather than try to correct the situation by increasing the tension of pulling away from center by inspiration, it is much easier and wiser to recondition the respiratory apparatus through the phase of expiration.

Expiration is known as the "passive" phase within respiration. To the musician, the word "passive" can be confusing because it is during this period of controlled release that he is traveling from "here to there" as he sings or plays an instrument. However, if the musician manages to associate the word "passive" with the playing released out of the impulse (sensed in inspiration) in suspension, he is saying the same thing as "traveling from here to there."

In the physical process of breathing, we are expiring correctly if we are pulling the body structure together from within, freeing the diaphragm, and readying it for its pistonlike movement in inspiration. We have been further assured by Miss Todd that

in the "passive phase" of the diaphragm action, during expiration, increased tonicity of the abdominal wall prepares the lower muscular mechanism for its next action—either in jumping or breathing.[10]

May we add "and in the next phrase of music"?

It has been proven in laboratories that voicing the sound of the letter "H" ties breathing and posture back to the center structure. Expiration normally occurs during the physical process of "hissing," which has this letter as its initial sound. Animals provide an illustration of hissing in that when they are engaged in fighting or in taking flight, they "hiss" and pull back and down through the spine to the earth. The pianist may attempt to achieve the same connected effect by hissing.

Human hissing is reconditioning for building a kinesthetic response for wholeness through the balanced center. The dynamic center, as a passageway for initiating a breathing rhythm synchronized with a structural rhythm, is the carrier of musical rhythmical impulses. (See Chapters VI and VII.)

As the structure draws together, a proper lever is made of the sit-bones, directing the line of force to the chair. The sit-bones are the live, balanced stance of sitting support for all movements of a free shoulder girdle and arms. Hissing correctly along the lengthened axis gives support to the spine as the ribs come down. Side pulls, which hamper the organization of energy for long-line movement, can be remedied by hissing correctly. One must be careful not to hiss against the spine, pushing the back outward and disturbing the alignment.

Hissing should be a part of all of the body readiness exercises

---

10 Todd, *The Thinking Body, op. cit.,* p. 259.

suggested in this thesis. Generalized, they include: From a balanced sitting position, hiss slowly, testing the ribs to see that they are folding gently along the long spinal axis. Allow the sternum to float up, and allow the two upper ribs to be lifted from above,

This student is demonstrating the proper "hissing" technique. As a result of this exercise, her ribs are folding close to the spine and the two forces are becoming established through the center.

thus freeing the shoulder girdle. The arms suspended from the balanced torso feel as though they are resting on flexible shock absorbers. The legs are drawn back into the leg sockets and are able to swing easily to any position which will accommodate the total line of balance.

There must be no blocked energy in the spine at any time. Every joint must be able to articulate. These suggestions are invaluable as preconditioning for the total rhythmic phases of breathing; namely, expiration, rest, and inspiration.

REST PHASE OF RESPIRATION

In the rhythmic cycle of normal respiration, nature has prepared a short but definite rest phase as a transition between expiration and inspiration. It is almost as though nature wishes to catch up with herself before the life force turns, or similarly, it often appears that the body has to catch up with the energy from within. The more effortlessly and quietly this changeover occurs, the more emotionally and physically stable is the condition within and the more ready one is to practice or play.

After one has breathed outward completely in the process of hissing, nature's rest phase is very noticeable. Because of the rest phase, one should not have to gasp for the incoming breath of inspiration.

At all times, the pianist should be able to sense an underlying base of support at the bench. As his body "collects" in the anticipation of initiating a rhythmic impulse, a movement always accompanied by the diaphragmatic muscle contraction for releasing motion, the mature performer does not lose his sense of an inner balance. It is essential that in training we have a knowledgeable kinesthetic awareness of a balanced transitional phase of rest between expiration and inspiration.

Nature's cycle of expiration, rest, and inspiration parallels the musician's experience in sensing a musical span of suspension, rest, and impulse within the onward progression into the next idea. When the respiratory cycle is synthesized within the musical span, the subconscious takes over in habitual response.

In order that music move living forms, there is always a sensation of alertness, release, and action to the peak; rest then follows. The genius is so innately rhythmical that if he were confronted with a teaching situation in which the problem centered around such an inner rhythmic blocking, he would probably be surprised and say, "Of course. Doesn't everyone sense this rhythmic cycle?"

There are always musicians who sense no rest within the rhythmic cycle and who push to the end of the span. There are also, however, those performers who simply "die on the vine." Both of these musical types are in error. Rest does not terminate in a dead impasse; rather, it is a vital cessation between expiration and inspiration.

INSPIRATION PHASE OF RESPIRATION

After expiration and the pause of rest that immediately follows it, the involuntary act of inspiration takes place naturally and completes the sequence of respiration. Inspiration is given a healthy impetus by the diaphragm's fullest trek downward accompanied by the expansion of the rib case and the stabilization of the lower accessory muscles in reciprocation.

While appreciating the consistency of nature's processes, the instrumentalist, in particular, will naturally wonder how the cycle of respiration can have any bearing upon transforming a "dry" performance into a creative one.

The simplest act by which to experience diaphragmatic inspiration is the sensation of a yawn. A yawn can be initiated and released in any degree of velocity. In training imagery and kinesthetic response to release energy which travels to the periphery of the body, we can yawn with "jet propulsion." There is a quick release of the diaphragmatic plunge which, acting as a "springboard," permeates the total body with energy. From this beginning we can become more specific: by sensing connection and inflation through the connective tissues, we experience a total lightweight body through the directed energy to the arches of the hand, to the feet, to the top of the head, or to the lower back. Completing this kinesthetic experience, one senses the entire body trailing through the pathway which the breath movement has created. The follow-through is a synthesized reality of inner and outer movement.

Technique, born of life itself, need not be confusing if imagery and terminology are within the scope of the student's understanding. Because breath is so intimately a part of all our inhibitions and vivifications affecting voluntary and involuntary response, some students at first are shy and reluctant to cooperate in breathing techniques. However, if the instructor presents breath training as objectively as he does a five-finger exercise, the student gradually overcomes any resistance to what he may view as an intrusion into "where he lives." No separation should be made, therefore, in teaching a process which will ultimately generate the musical carrying-line and the kinesthetic experience to release it.

Yawning correctly, we are reminded that the action of the diaphragmatic contraction is always ahead of the expansion of the ribs. The ribs never lock, and the diaphragm does not hold and "set itself." The breastbone remains high and still. There is no raising and holding of the shoulders. The inner balance of the two forces maintains a quiet center.

In the use of the diaphragm as a "springboard" to release the sensed stored energy of the rhythmic impulse, we train consciously until that time when the subconscious can take over. Musical units of short or long duration, such as motive, meter, and phrase, are impulsed and spent in spacetime. The gathering of the force is influenced by mood, tempo, depth, intensity, inner phrasing, and all of the factors which a sensitive musician responds to and desires from within. Out of the release of inspiration comes the suspended act of playing which the skilled musician controls by the supportive components existing through the phase of expiration. Because of his response to sound and rhythm, the performer senses in proportion the necessary stored energy which is finally released and the controlled duration of the suspensatory space-time fulfillment. He also senses the tiny interim of rest between finishing one unit and initiating another.

Any musician attuned to the subtle distinction between a performance with the synthesization of inner and outer motion and one without it instinctively senses when the movements of articulation have been deserted by the power of the breath. He is aware of an insecure rhythmic progression which is usually augmented by arms and hands whacking away with dry, crisp sounds. Can this be the underlying reason why some performers do not enjoy playing or listening to others play Bach?

And when does the teacher have time in the piano lesson to bridge the academic symbol and the living performance? Of course, time is always a problem, but very gradually through imagery, guidance, and actual practice, the student becomes what he images. The instructor who has concepts founded and rooted in life's processes is able to accelerate the solving of his students' problems with both assurance and satisfaction.

VII. Rhythm—The Relationship Between the Musical Idea and the Carrying-Line

It appears that the musician creates rhythmic "life forms" from nothing. Yet thoughts, feelings, and pure abstractions which are nondescriptive can be externalized as "sounding forms in motion." Can it be that out of nothing man has partial access to understanding and to experiencing nature's forces? Nothing is everything in embryo. Man did not create the substance from which rhythm evolves. He merely discovers nature's concealed and partly revealed processes through experience.

The musical idea of the whole composition is "caught and felt" from within through the conception of the composer or performer when he first considers a work. Once the musical shape is felt, the composition exists in embryo. The carrying-line exists in motion. The vivification of this impression varies with the innate ability of the individual to absorb it both mentally and emotionally and to respond to it organically.

Cora Belle Hunter clarified for me the concept of the rhythmic carrying-line which unifies the total musical content with the total body-mind organism. She also helped me to experience it. This statement by no means implies that I am able to retain this ideal condition at all times in my own playing. It does mean, though, that I have found the principle indispensable and directly relevant.

The carrying-line is the embodiment of an invisible motion

"idea." It is the carrier of myriad musical components within the greater musical content. Among these coexistent integral factors are: mood, tempo, rhythm, melody, harmony, texture, meter, note values, dynamics, gradations, nuances, contrasts, similarities, and repetitions. Every composition has its own identity through the unification of its component elements sensed in the ongoing rhythmic surge toward the goal. As the goal is reached, whether in part or as a whole, form is established.

Nothing enters the creation of music without being ordered by a governing principle. The entry of sounds is regulated by the governing principles of melody and harmony, and the motion forward is regulated by the governing principle of rhythm. As Dr. Schlieder said so often, "The essence of rhythm is the preparation of a new event by the ending of a previous one." [1]

The artist should not be expected to delve into defining what he thinks he feels any more than the child can explain why he is soothed and lulled to sleep by the rocking motion of a cradle. I think immediately of what happened to an elderly lady taking a music lesson when she, encouraged to do so, jubilantly proceeded to "swing in a rhythm." Heretofore, her only childhood musical experience was to have her conscientious instructor stop her in measure two to clean up minute detail. The artist, of course, would not have allowed this to happen. It is said that Handel, while writing *The Messiah,* could not let go of his pen, even to eat. His idea and fundamental movement kept surging toward completion.

I shall never forget watching Walter Russell sculpture the bust of George Washington. Never did his eyes leave the figure unfolding from the slab of material. His tools were handed to him by his assistants so that his concentration would not be compromised by movements peripheral to his sculpture. The artist is "drawn into the idea" and is carried totally in a body-feeling-rhythmic progression. From these three different sources, one may conclude that music—and indeed all art—contains a basic rhythm and is the source of its own organic unity.

---

[1] Frederick William Schlieder, class notes.

Looping the lines of force into one central carrying-line.

Dr. Schlieder assures us of art's organic rhythm in this way:

> This feeling of something moving forward in geared motion is the expression of one's life force, one's vital energy. Rhythm is therefore ordered vitality, because rhythm is a feeling and feeling is only possible where there is life. Time forms are an emotional and spiritual experience.[2]

The philosopher Suzanne Langer voices the meaning similarly:

> The commanding form of a piece of music contains its basic rhythm, which is at once the source of its organic unity and its total feeling. The concept of rhythm as a relation between tensions rather than as a matter of equal divisions of time (i.e. meter) makes it quite comprehensible that harmonic progressions, resolutions of dissonances, directions of "running" passages, and "tendency tones" in melody all serve as rhythmic agents.[3]

To these comments Henri Poincaré adds:

> . . . the idea that we take our own body as an instrument of measurement, in order to construct space—not the geometrical space, neither a space of pure representation, but a space belonging to an "instinctive geometry" . . . .[4]

Science assists in furnishing concepts which strengthen the kinesthetic awareness of "instinctive geometry." Rhythmic motion is generated within through the balanced behavior of the two forces through the dynamic axis. Science also declares that in a condition of polarization, energy generates vertically through the axis and disperses horizontally. This concept is directly relevant to the analogy we have discussed.

We have explained that motion is initiated through diaphragmatic action and sit-bone resistance to the bench, and that it is

---

[2] Frederick William Schlieder, class notes.

[3] Susanne K. Langer, *Feeling and Form: A Theory of Art* (New York, Charles Scribner's Sons, 1953), p. 129.

[4] Henri Poincaré, quoted in Langer, *op. cit.,* p. 91.

spent in released suspension. Because of the vertical axis and the gravitational pull to the earth, the pianist is kinesthetically aware that motion is initiated in a vertical direction.

Upon completion of a finished cycle, the new cycle is sensed and the diaphragm is looped in the service of the rhythm. The movement of the diaphragm triggers the tension to be spent in an ordered dispersion through the duration of the rhythmic unit. The follow-through from the vertical push-off and from the horizontal placement of the articulative patterns upon the keyboard is sensed in curvature. The "instinctive geometry" of which Henri Poincaré speaks as not being "a space of pure representation" is now an organic experience responsible for the birth and establishment of the circumference of the basic form as it follows through in "outer space" over the instrument.

We hope to clarify the idea that one does not necessarily give a push-off from the base of the chair to instigate the first beat of every measure. The beat may appear in the middle of a measure or phrase to stress a dynamic effect; the music dictates when it is necessary to initiate a musical unit from the structural base. The breath, however, can with the slightest activity outwit the pull of gravity and revitalize the ongoing motion. Again we state that the breath does not dictate the course of the music; rather, it is the need of the individual to perpetuate the organic vitality of the music. It has been suggested that the idea and enactment of the sound of "ah" are enough to cause a diaphragmatic spring.

Children or adults may experience the ongoing spiral phase of impulse and suspension through the tossing of balloons. All principles heretofore discussed, except for the keyboard articulations, apply here. When done skillfully, and when gravity is *serving* rather than overpowering the center balance, balloon-tossing is valuable experience in sensing a balanced center and in experiencing impulse and suspension, conditions which require a very exact sensitivity to the various changing moods and tempos of the rhythm. This activity is excellent in sensing the long phrase which extends farther and farther outward in suspension.

The difference between the "phase of suspension out of the impulse" and the "state of suspension" which the body enjoys from

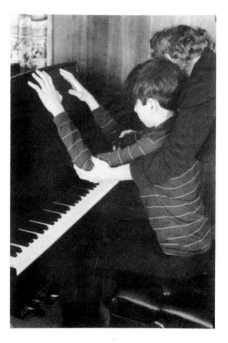

The teacher helps the student assimilate the arms into the total rhythmic spiral. The student feels that they are within his "orbit." The arms and sit-bones are aligned and connected.

the support of the base may need a remark of clarification. Actually, in the ideal state the body is always suspended and is ready to adjust to the slightest nuance or variant within the ongoing motion.

A performer who is tremendously gifted rhythmically is one who senses rhythmic balance in the changing states of impulse and suspension. However, it takes an individual with less sensitivity than the artist to give attention to and interpretative evidence for sense data. The artist senses in wholeness and works from vision. The scientist can assist in partially explaining what the artist senses in wholeness.

Every impulse is an angle of attention. The aural image, inciting the anticipated motion, the gathering of the force to be released, the traveling to the peak, the turning of the force, and the stealthily merged and completed phase of suspension are all timed within an indivisible wholeness of motion within the cycle.

Two different relevant images for these experiences are readily apparent. The first of these is the type of water sprinkler in which water is directed through the vertical spout as it spirals and sprays the grass horizontally. The other which immediately comes to mind is that of the skillful golfer who said to me as he made a long drive, "I always hit the ball at the lowest point on the way up."

There are many tiny, varied spirals within the basic form unit which complete the articulative technical variants. These tiny movements are finished as they "tuck into" the one "great rhythm." Whatever the composer's intention and the performer's interpretation of the basic rhythmic form, the music is carried in wholeness from the base of the torso and is kept alive through the spark of the breath. The completed cycle travels to the keyboard and returns to itself at the base. Such is the unquestioned matrix of the composition.

Suspension within the basic form of a composition can be likened to skating or dancing, where one floats through space and comes back to earth long enough for another propulsion forward. We are no longer earthbound in experiencing the limitations of a flat energy level. The unfortunate child who is never awakened beyond the experience of a plunk-plunk, note-by-note progression is justified in "hating" piano lessons. He has had no difficulty in sensing the "imp" in the impulse when he jumps rope, and no doubt he has been thrilled by the motion of riding on a Ferris wheel or a bicycle. He hears the bird who instinctively sings through an impulse. He could agree with the pianist Alec Templeton when he expressed over the radio, "Tonight I'm on the beam," but unfortunately this sensation is never a part of his own musical experience.

As parents and teachers know, students identify easily with their pets. "Pant like a dog" brings a lusty diaphragmatic response. "Hist! Hist! Be still!" is an easy exclamation by which the student may sense a quick diaphragmatic action which can be directed to his total pianistic experience. It may mean a rhythmic impulse, a quick stress, or a staccato release.

Nursery rhymes and poems which vary in mood and rhythm contain a storehouse of examples to be linked with musical rhythm and breath. The stressed syllables are "sent" from the diaphragm, and the weaker syllables or words "float" in the feeling of suspension.

It is imperative that the student be aware of the note values as relative vibratory entities within a larger sweep of geared motion. (See Chapter VIII on symbols.) The inability of the standardized printed symbol to stimulate vital organic organization and response is a common barrier to the total performance. The question arises: "Is it possible to disclose a symbol representative of a symbol?" In other words, "Can music which is symbolic of thought and feeling be adequately symbolized by notation denoting sound and motion?" The musician's immediate answer is to drill until the symbol can present none other than the desired response.

We feel justified in using the image of an ongoing spiral around and through an axis. It seems most symbolically representative of the invisible form of musical progression. It is indicative of the blend of the two forces in curvature, establishing the all-inclusive carrying-line of musical continuity.

SPIRIT AND EMOTION

Once or twice during the extended career of the unsung music instructor, a student appears who is so intuitively gifted that his emotive faculties tune immediately to the inherent spiritual values within the music. He is both eager and willing to muse over his chances for success as a musician. Acknowledging within himself that the Creator who bestowed the gift can also chart its course, the teacher accepts the challenge of working with the gifted student. He then creates opportunities and unselfishly encourages the student to seek counsel beyond the instructor's own limitations.

While pondering over the future of his students, the teacher may wonder whether it is something in music that kindles emotion, or whether it is something within us that follows the heart of the music. He instructs the student in ways to channel emotion mentally and physically, and assists in awakening his response to the lifeless symbols of the composer which lie encased in silence. The mystery of music is at least partially solved to their mutual satisfaction through the experience of unifying music, composer, and performer.

The teacher holds the key to much of what his student will eventually grasp about the essence of music. Through his good taste he attempts to objectify the gifts of nature, all of the "voices of earth and heaven," that can be identified as ready sources of wonder communicable through feeling. Each student is free to respond to these musical stimuli. He retains his own identity to the point that the same sounds which arouse laughter within him may entreat tears in another. The teacher's skill and ultimate musical worth lie in his ability to awaken the dramatic forces of life at any level. It is true, however, that the teacher cannot command responses from his students. He can only guide and awaken.

The mind trains what feeling has given it. Meaning and response constitute awakening. The mind easily becomes bored with the steps that are necessary to earn the physical and aural response to symbols. If the flames of emotion leading to the student's goal are kept alive, the burden of the symbol will disappear in the shadow of his efforts.

Rhythm is control over emotion. Reason is selective and can, with the help of the spirit, choose the height of aspiration which it serves. If the response to spirit and emotion within the body as the "temple" is uninspired, the musician's performance and musical experience will be less than total or enjoyable. Bach reflected his own seriousness and concerns by writing" . . .S.D.G. (*Soli Deo Gloria:* 'to God alone the glory') . . ." [5] at the conclusion of all of his more serious music.

---

[5] Hans T. David and Arthur Mendel, eds., *The Bach Reader: A Life of Johann Sebastian Bach in Letters and Documents* (New York, W. W. Norton, 1966), p. 32.

VIII. Discovering the Symbol

Within the mechanical process of learning symbols lies the discipline that leads to creative musical growth. In fact, all training is negligible unless we can develop a chain-lightning response to the multitudinous signs as living, vibrating units.

A sound is an event occurring in space-time. It derives its meaning in its relationship to other vibrating sounds and to pitch, duration, and intensity.

A note is a picture of a sound. "Holding" a note is impossible. Rather, as a young student said, "We move through the space of a half note."

Rests are silent motion.

Fortzandos, accents, syncopations, stresses, and fermatas are all to be considered and experienced in proportionate degrees of inner dynamics. From the second that the symbol is introduced, there is a responsibility for the instructor to impart understanding and to awaken a vital response in his student to each small part and to the whole. Artur Schnabel has said that every sound should first be desired from within. [1]

The immediate symbols requiring kinesthetic response may be divided into three classifications: (1) aural, (2) motion between the parts and the whole, and (3) the palpable shapes of the instrument to be played. Tonal aspects, as important as it is to awaken them, are usually given last consideration. They ride in the stream of motion.

In the momentum of establishing a performance in the average studio, "ear training" and the association with the written symbol

---

[1] Schnabel, *op. cit.* p. 132.

usually have to wait. The tactile (hand-shape patterns) hold the limelight in many of the present piano courses because emphasis is currently on fluent reading of the symbols and on the immediate playing response on the keyboard. This emphasis is most unfortunate because it gives mechanics more importance than playing music.

The second requisite to the playing process (either mechanical or creative) is the ability to sense measured motion which carries the sound and the articulative patterns. It is therefore imperative to establish an unquestionable response to a steady ongoing progression of changing note values.

The student is "bopping" the individual sounds, thereby connecting inner and outer controls.

There is much division among teachers as to the value of counting aloud. If counting remains only an intellectual voicing, why bother? We need to count with a vitality that causes us to lift and give off energy. Energy affects breath. If one "bops" * each sound from the diaphragm, control of the parts will be established. The issue is not whether one prefers words or numerals or just plain "bops." We know of no other reliable way to control speed than to deliberately bop every single note value, thereby tying the finger release to the breath stream. One should not release a finger until the diaphragm has first initiated the impulse.

Many students with very good "ears" respond to musical stimuli by singing, but the response is often accompanied by a weak rhythmic current. They may resist the teacher's attempts to help them feel energy because it takes effort to be vital. The student's greatest need is often his point of greatest resistance. To further ensure the kindling of inner vitality, the teacher may direct the student's power through his fingers "in the air" as he (the student) continues the verbalization. The instructor must be sure that the student does not push with the small muscles. He should merely swing his fingers vitally.

The much-used activities of clapping, tapping, walking, and swinging may be helpful in establishing disciplined note-by-note progressions, but they should be recognized as activities and little more. At the same time that the teacher is encouraging these activities, he can be suggesting the techniques presented in Chapter II to give his student the sensation of existing "within his own orbit." The student will be assimilating and directing his body parts from a vital center.

The metronome as a noncreative discipline is used in most studios. It has its place, to be sure; but in giving the student a fair analysis, he should know when he is assembling his "flat-level tools" and when he is using his "dynamic tools" in his steps toward making music. The metronome can be responsible for destroying any semblance of lever suspension in a creative flow of geared motion.

-----

* See glossary.

Nature is as meticulous in the formation and function of each tiny cell as she is in the whole creation. Similarly, any teacher who has had a smattering of experience knows that the response to the tiniest note value has to be ingrained in the total learning process. In my eagerness to bypass the tedious drilling of note values during my early years of teaching, I found I was most unhappy when the student was on the verge of playing the composition. Truly enough, the playing was often spirited, but it was sloppy.

There are many patterns within two-four, three-four, and four-four vocabularies and their subdivisions alone. Today's varieties of measure lengths and the contemporary preoccupation with changing meter should not baffle the performer if he is thoroughly trained to sense the behavior of the basic measurements. If he senses through creative motion the phases of starting, continuing, and finishing a unit of geared motion, he is progressing toward his goal. However, to be master of the whole, one must be master of the part. The "betweenness" is crucial. "Betweenness" is realized in the ongoing motion by the the musician as he unfolds the rhythmic form in performance.

SYMBOLS IN A DIFFERENT LIGHT

With gradual building in the consciousness, with experience of a center support, and through continual practice of the octave exercise, the youngest student is able to sustain suspended tones in an impulsed measure motion. The most elementary pattern suitable for practicing purposes is that of two-four time, notated as two quarter notes. Establishing a balanced suspended torso, the student plays a four-measure phrase sensing a released impulse through the first beats of each measure and a suspension through all the second beats. He says and feels, "Send, float," in each measure.

Thus far the student has sensed only measure motion. As a learning step it is wise to have him pause after the "float" in one unit in order to sense the chair "holding him" as a point of finishing. Almost immediately, the cycle can be extended in space as a four-measure phrase.

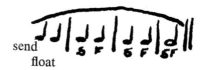

The carrying-line, tempo, and rhythm are represented by symbols in an ongoing motion.

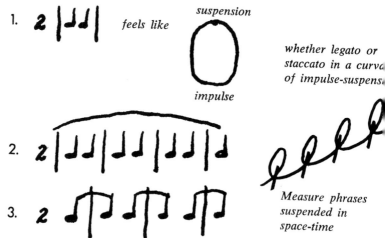

The phrases which begin on the first beat of the measure are sensed as starting with the push-off from the sit-bones and breath. Phrases which begin on the second beat of a measure may have more feeling of suspension with only a tiny breath impulse. The music at hand dictates all of these subtleties.

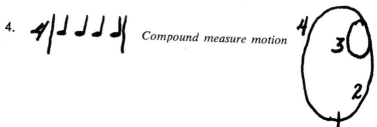

5. *The following figures are merely primitive symbols of motion which the music may dictate:*

Shallow curvature due to a fast tempo. Short notation.

Deep curvature due to a slow tempo. Longer notation.

Center sensed within

Center sensed within

This most elementary musical experience extends to the shaping of longer phrases and inner phrasing, both of which are inclusive of small motives and patterns. Circles within circles of completed musical units evolve into the feeling of form.

SYMBOLS AS A CLUE TO MUSICAL FORM

The ethical performer must rely on the clues which the composer has given him on the printed page. Very often, these clues have been seriously tampered with by editors, in which case the performer must consult various editions of the work or the opinion of musicians he respects. Occasionally through much exposure to literature at large, he may increase his sensitivity to the insoluble problem. The printed page, however, must be preserved.

It has been evident in various seminars taught by eminent teachers that the one great gap between the academic and the artistic performance can be bridged only by the ability of the instructor to give the player the concept of the all-inclusive carrying-line. In simple terminology, instructors have helped to unify spatial parts into a spatial whole, and have "given the piece a shape." For a flash of time, the performer is lifted in spirit, and he lauds the teacher with well-deserved praise. But, upon returning to the next session, the student seems to have lost his sense of unity. Regardless of the amount of time between sessions and the changes of composition, the old, fragmentary patterns reappear. The student in this case had no imagery with which to evaluate through his own efforts and to approximately approach the intent of the composer.

The carrying-line or movement which the body initiates and spins from the center releases the component elements or framework of the composition. In reverse, the component elements (rhythm, melody, harmony, texture, dynamics, and color) determine the controlled carrying-line as musical form evolves.

Rhythm is the most important single musical factor. Rhythm, tempo, and time are synthesized into a musical whole, but each carries its distinctive features with it. Tempo, together with rhythm, is dependent upon the interacting intention of the component parts. If any element is vying for supremacy beyond the composer's intention, the tempo will be distorted.

Musical meaning, which is evidenced in the carrying-line and in the rhythmic motion that enfolds the various musical components, reveals the character of the composition. This character is the "more-than-sum" of the elements.

Mozart simply cannot sound like Rachmaninoff if the carrying line is determined by the framework of the composition in auditory, spatially sensed parts within the whole. Who has not heard a renowned pianist on his "off-day" play a Scarlatti sonata with the same flourish of gestures and intensity of tone with which he might play a Prokofieff composition? Of course, the newspaper critic is immediately alert to this fatal sameness, and the pianist is accordingly reminded of his inadequacy in print the next morning.

As a rule, the composer aids the performer by choosing the most significant and traditional symbol to notate his composition. Could one envision Grieg writing *The Butterfly* in half notes? The performer is well on the way to a convincing performance if he has chosen music written by a sensitive composer and catches the character, form, and rhythmic units in impulse and suspension. There is always a basic motion regardless of the myriad divisions, stresses, accents, and so forth, within this motion.

SYMBOLS AND MUSICAL MEANING

A. *"Facility" Compositions*

PAPILLON.
(BUTTERFLY.)

evised and fingered by
W.ᵐ *Scharfenberg.*

EDVARD GRIEG.

Allegro grazioso. (♩ = 132.)

PIANO.

The title of Grieg's composition is descriptive of its character. In a tempo mark such as "Allegro grazioso," one would expect to find light, graceful, and in this case short phrases expressive of a butterfly. The continuing sixteenth-note values indicate his light, soaring antics. The inverted chord structures and the chromatic ascending passages enhance the feeling of suspension. It is most obvious that the character of the music is conducive to developing a lightweight body that would erase any tendency to drop dead weight into the keys.

As always, there should be no reaching ahead with the levers. The motion of the carrying-line, initiated from the sit-bone base with a diaphragmatic impulse, can be imaged as spun out and traveling in fine elliptical spirals. The "push-off" from the base would yield to the frequency of the breath impulses in this light, suspended composition. The arms, supported and connected through the torso, are sensed as looped to the diaphragmatic impulses. The small articulations are completed through undulation, rotation, and "swinging" fingers. The fingers remain very close to the keys and need only the slightest flexion.

Tiny "ah" breaths before the first (and possibly before the third) beat of each measure help to maintain vitality throughout the suspension. One should be certain that the melodic chord (A–E–C#–A) on the fourth beat of measure one is carried forward in suspension, and that the balanced center line of the body is poised, ready to employ the tiny "down and under" curve to initiate the impulse at the beginning of the second measure. The printed accents in measure two can be ugly if one does not yield to the rhythmic flow established in measure one. The melodic figure can remain distinct without overaccentuation.

It is helpful to prepare the "inner space feeling" by playing only the first note of the first and third beats in tempo while directing one's awareness to the sense of traveling silently through the second and fourth beats. The performer should gradually fill in the sounds only after there is no feeling of "making" the articulations. These articulations are released in the feeling of the onward-geared motion through the center of the torso.

If the student is having difficulty sustaining the curve through the center, and if his top arm is not suspended, the teacher may assist him by telescoping the forearm into the top arm and the top arm into the arm socket. These motions give him the feeling of the arm in one piece. He can also give him the feeling of the "two forces" through his center by supporting his total arm and at the same time giving a thrust toward the sit-bone base as a point of resistance and support.

B. *Mood Pieces or Lyrics*

The title of Chopin's piece is again indicative of its mood and content. This composition is characteristic of the melodic and harmonic beauty for which Chopin is known.

It is relatively easy to establish a long-line, measure-phrase motion of four-four time; that is, out of the released tension of the first and third beats flow the second and fourth. It is significant, too, that Chopin notated the composition in twelve-eight time because of the substance and color of the harmonic background accompanying the lyric quality of the melody. Harmonic and

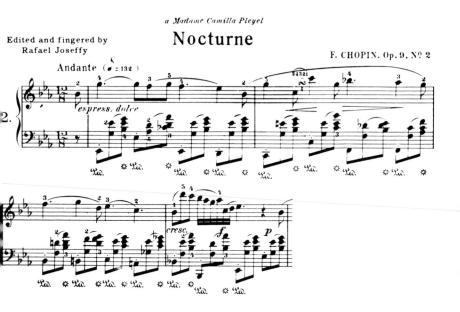

melodic intensity do not deteriorate because one is traveling in the suspended energy of the tiny impulsed *one's* and *three's*.

The temporary musical goals of the "Nocturne" are being met as they progress to the ultimate peak, which in this composition appears in the fourth from the last measure. In practice, at least, the breath can be used in the smallest of palpitations through the individual groups of triplet eighths in the accompaniment. Also, giving the tiniest impulse to the second eighth in the group of three eighths stimulates vitality, not only in the accompaniment but also in the sustained melodic tones. The composition must remain balanced.

The impulses have to be organized within us quickly enough to sustain the curvature. A total lever connection from base to fingertips is necessary for carrying the long-line rhythm. Imagining the articulation and the arm as a violinist's bow may be helpful.

Any teacher who has taught this composition to several students must have been faced with the problems of "pumping arms," ugly accents, and excess sentimentality. Sensing balanced energy (the flexible "pull down" and "push up") through the fine center line and allowing the breath to release and feed the suspensions can help the student to quiet and direct the "too busy" gestures within the motion of the whole.

Much skill and sensitivity are required in controlling the repetitive themes, variations, nuances, and dynamics. If one establishes a basic, creative motion, he may play the "Nocturne" without distortion.

C. Deep Rhythmic Curvatures

It is merely coincidental that the three excerpts which we have chosen for different content and rhythmic curvature happen to be in the same measurement of four. Any musical measurement would be suitable for teaching purposes.

Bach's well-known "Adagio" from the *Organ Toccata in C Major,* with its rich, harmonic, open texture, requires the support of the breath for the deep impulses which trigger and sustain the

ADAGIO
from Organ Toccata in C major, No.1
by J. S. BACH

Adapted for Piano
by MYRA HESS

Adagio: il Canto sempre legatissimo

use of the accessory muscles of the deep pelvis. This organic response aids in supporting and continuing the intensity between impulses. The flowing eighth-note bass and the "tucked-in" (but not slighted) melodic dotted-sixteenths and thirty-seconds are clearly interpreted within the wider, deeper cycles of curvature. Maintaining energy to the top of the head aids in retaining the balance of the two forces that is necessary to the dignity of the composition.

The inversion of the E major chord on the third beat of measure one is indicative of a higher energy lift in the extending suspension. This statement does not mean that the passage is necessarily less intense. The roots, inversions, and harmonic suspensions are indicative of the need to image and channel the released energy for the response to emotive color. The torso is capable of supporting the long-line terraced phrases within the desired dynamics.

Precautions should be taken to keep the cohesive power through the center instead of allowing the horizontal distance between the octave intervals in the bass to take over. The necessity for maintaining the vertical power is unquestioned in conveying the majesty and depth of this composition.

IX. From Pulse to Pattern

PIANISTIC PATTERNS

Technique, in the larger artistic sense, implies "how" to reach the goal through the control of the parts (the pianistic patterns) within the total rhythm. Technical patterns are therefore important because they spell out musical textures which are the framework of the form.

In many studios, the idea still persists that ease and beauty of playing will as a matter of course emerge from hours of drilling, which include exercises ranging from slow to maximum speed through such pianistic patterns as scales and arpeggios. Surely, all will agree that it is necessary to think, hear, and shape keyboard vocabularies in a chain-lightning response, and, because we differ in the speed with which we assimilate and control movement, slow motion is not discouraged. However, the student should be told why he is going about his practice in a specified way. What does he hope to accomplish?

1. Does he need to clarify the mental and aural picture of every future sound in the moving line?
2. Is he carefully thinking of and placing an exact finger on a specific key?
3. Is he observing the movements which are possible in the interaction of articulation?
4. Is he listening for the sound which a particular touch produces, or a certain pedal effect?

When the student has actually *earned* a kinesthetic response to the keyboard vocabularies and from the principles of the wholeness of rhythmic motion can extend his control from center through the articulation, he will not find it necessary to spend hours acquiring facility and speed. His challenge lies in his ability to move the pianistic patterns in the motion of the whole. We are not ignoring the factors of motivation, industry, and potential, which can hasten or retard the skill involving kinesthetic memory. As the student matures he, no doubt, will spend an endless amount of time perfecting the balanced motion between the impulse and the spending of it which will result in clarity and in the placement of every living sound within the phrase.

The words "weight" and "energy," as they are employed by instructors of music, have different meanings. A demonstration given by a teacher who "acted out" every point she wished to make led me to investigate her theory further. She let her arm hang at her side from her shoulder and said, "They say I play with weight. Now please tell me, how can I lift my arm to the keys? You notice, I must see myself doing it, and then there must be energy to move it."

Scientists claim that they cannot explain the mystery of matter and energy, but it is obvious to most of us that the artist's whole performance is conceived from within and released through organized energy. The question will arise regarding the point at which the weight focuses and rests in a legato progression, especially in a slow tempo, with long-note values, or in a condition where one voice is sustaining and the others are moving simultaneously. Tone is imaged before the release of energy to the keys, and the overtones are sensed as "finishing" out the motion of the fundamental tone. In a legato touch, it is necessary for the hands to remain on the slightly depressed keys, but the sensation is that the rhythmic line is continuing onward through the fingertips. This does not imply that the hands must slide, wiggle, or try to fill in the time by pushing to the bottom of the key-bed. *Playing happens in the state of suspension.* We are not held by the support of the keys and should not envision a weighted production.

Nature has designed the sit-bone base, sensed in the support of the gravitational pull to the earth, as the resting place for the playing process. The teacher may wish to experiment with this concept using Chopin's "Prelude," *Opus 28,* no. 20. At first, the pianist can allow his weight to rest on the keys after producing each chord. Then he may play the chords again in the pulsed, sensed rhythm, feeling the cycle of impulse, chord release, and motion between each succeeding chord. He senses the resting at the base during the entire rhythmic cycle. In the first try, the pianist was using only one of the two forces: the downward, mechanical force. It takes the interaction of the two forces—mechanical and neuromuscular—to create rhythm.

Faulty playing can stem predominantly from:

1.   Confusion in aural imagery, and confusion in the execution of time units.
2.   A slow response to the tactile imagery of the pianistic patterns and their preparation within kinesthetic memory.
3.   Inadequate support to carry the top arm, forearm, and finger articulations to the point of key release within the rhythm.

If the pianist is to play a scale, a chord, or an arpeggio, his mind pictures and his trained hand lends itself to a pianistically shaped pattern. If he has heard one major scale, he has heard twelve, but that in itself is no assurance that he has earned the "pattern sense" of the twelve. Even if his center control is secure enough to carry a four-octave range skillfully, he must still learn to handle the patterns and to perfect the small adjustments.

Whether the patterns are moved as repeats, steps, or skips, or through degrees of staccato or legato touches, they are carried through the sensation of the balance of the two forces through the center. The two forces merge in the spinning out of the curved rhythm; they control the timing and placement of the articulations on the keys. (The word "timing" is not to be confused with the phrase "note values.") If the training of the tactile patterns has been unrelated to the moving line and the student grabs, yanks, and drops his hands, he has probably reached a point of rigidity which a leading psychologist would call a slow-moving fixation and a condition of tenseness. [1]

---

[1] Wells, *op. cit.,* p. 334.

USES OF THE OCTAVE
IN ESTABLISHING A BASIC CONTROL

The student of any age who can span an octave should begin his piano experience with the solid octave exercise. With the aid of the teacher, the youngest child may be given a grace note—

The teacher is assisting a young student who has less than an octave span. As a result of support given to the top arm and forearm, the hand remains gently open as the elbow flexes in the octave pattern.

octave procedure. In the exercise, the teacher places his hand gently on the student's shoulder, a movement which helps him sense resistance through the center to the base of support. With

This student is eight years old and can span an octave. He plays octave exercises effortlessly.

In the octave exercise, power is initiated from the sit-bones through the top arm, forearm, hand, and fingers to the keys. This student has an unusually long top arm and had to learn to support it through center.

the other hand, the teacher lifts and supports his student's top arm until the latter can retain and sense the total connected arm through the balance of the two forces. With the right hand, to the vital saying of "Ta," the student plays the lower key of the octave as a grace note with the thumb. As he plays the top key with the fifth finger, the student says "dum" ("Ta-dum"). This exercise can be done by rote.

As always, action is initiated from the sit-bone base. "Ta-dum" springs from a tiny breath impulse. The side of the body that is not in action should not be devitalized. The left hand imitates the right hand, and soon both hands will be able to reverse the action from the fifth finger to the thumb. As soon as possible, the stunt is done with both hands and the student is well on the way to sensing *the torso carrying the two arms*. In the very beginning, it is best to use only three or four consecutive octaves at a time when working with a young student. While the student is becoming physically aware of wholeness, it is important to remind him of the natures of the impulse ("send"), the suspension ("float"), and the rest phases. The ear follows the progression of the changing tone. The hand should be opened gently at all times.

Within the experience of the octave cycle, the repetitive reflex action is easily established and "tucked into" the rhythm. The supported top arm is quiet and is stabilized by the torso. The most

EXERCISE FOR THE HAND
WITH LESS THAN AN OCTAVE SPAN

THE SOLID OCTAVE

CHROMATIC OCTAVES IN THE FRAMEWORK
OF THE DIMINISHED SEVENTH CHORD

Right or Left Hand: Octave or octaves apart

noticeable action in the repeated octave occurs just below the elbow joint within the forearm. The extended line of articulation through the wrist and hand and fingers upon the keys merely reflects the vibrations of the key-level action. All of the joints are closely connected, but if they were tested, all of them would be free to react.

Repetitive action must be consistent through the balanced key level of tone. Picture, for example, a stone skimming over the water. The air meets the water and the water meets the air. The stone skims through the two elements. If the arm is not supported through the two forces, it may hold up and out with the shoulder muscles or drive into the key-bed. Like the golfer who, under similar conditions, would dig up the turf or top the ball, the pianist will crash into the key-bed or only superficially touch the key. We can easily reduce the sensation of width in the hand span by applying the repetitive control to decreasing intervals, for example, to sevenths, to sixths, to fifths, and so on, until we arrive at the smallest interval, the second, out of which the thrill evolves.

The balanced line of force which travels through the hand span is the key to molding chord shapes. Chord shapes are, of course, determined by the individual's hand structure. When the hand is able to shape the chord, the relationship of the segments to the repetitive reflexes through the joints functions in a state of wholeness through the progression.

The forces are balanced and centered through the arch of the hand.

Because of the balanced pianist's sense of control, it is natural and relatively easy for him to sense and free the necessary articulations of undulation and rotation. Tone releases have been sensed at key level through the control of the two forces. One can now direct the articulations through the dynamic axis of the arm and hand which frees the fingers.

One test for the instructor to make repeatedly is to see that the top arm, sensed at the elbow tip, is initiated, supported, and aligned with the sit-bones through the torso. If this unity does not exist, the forearm and hand will be pulling somewhere along the alignment. The condition of the "one" stabilizing and freeing the "two" arms can now support the multiple activities of the ten fingers.

Putting into action the statement that " 'One' carries 'two,' 'two' carry 'ten,' " one can observe that the octave pattern lends itself most easily to this cycle of wholeness. The line of force through the hand span in the octave position is adequate to meet the keyboard. The octave pattern simplifies the changing of finger articulations.

While the student is growing and building a center control, he is not limited in the choice of materials suitable to his advancement and emotional satisfaction. He is being trained to stabilize and to move the smaller articulations within the greater control of melodic and harmonic patterns. Pieces constructed of pentachords, chord accompaniments, and skipping patterns now have a basis of control. Rotational, undulating, and repetitive movements are coordinated and timed in the rhythmic cycle and are gradually ushered in from the balanced center to the periphery.

Two stunts are valuable in awakening the sensation of "looping" the extremities of the keyboard into the center of the playing area. The glissando provides a perfect beginning because to execute it easily, one has to "ride" in the balanced see-saw relationship of key to hammer. If the student presses too deeply in the suspended continuity, he is "grounded." For greatest success with the glissando, the total arm, which follows the torso, should be allowed to follow the line of the body to the ends of the fingers. After this exercise is successfully performed "hands separately," then the student should do it with both hands in either parallel or contrary motion up and down the keyboard. Another exercise for developing kinesthetic awareness from the center of the keyboard to both extremities is to "skip-flip" octaves, one octave apart, without the use of the eyes. Few find this exercise an easy one.

For many pianists, trills are extremely difficult. Through the conditioning of repetitive intervals established in the choice of a second, the pianist may allow his fingers to articulate from the unbroken vibrating current traveling through the arm. He must be certain that the sit-bones are supporting the arm and that the tiny undulating, rotational interaction through the dynamic axis is neither "shut off" nor out of proportion. The pianist will find the

With the body following through from the point of resistance at the sit-bones, the glissando is directed through to the extremities of the keyboard. The two forces are balanced in the suspension.

trill easier to execute if he first rotates the octave and graduates the intervals down to the second. Trills should always be practiced in impulsed groups, and the pianist should be consciously aware of the points at which the pattern begins and ends. He should "bop" with the breath until the repetitions are too fast to "bop" the individual sound. The sensations should then be transferred to a larger wave.

PATTERNS REQUIRING EXTENSION

The same problems exist in all patterns which are extended on the keyboard. Arpeggios and scales are included in this category. After a group of keys has been successively covered and articulated under the hand in any pattern, including the frequently used scale and arpeggio, skill is required to extend the pattern up and down the keyboard without disturbing the tonal-rhythmic flow. Many pianists seem determined to connect and hold with the small muscles of the fingers in making these transitions. Not only do they reach ahead with small muscles, but they also pull the arm up and out of the power stream, a movement which detaches their support from base. To get back into the flow of power, the arm, hand, and thumb usually bump or grab.

The balance that is the result of the interaction of the down and up forces through the balanced center continues as potential power through the levers. As we experience the movement of getting "from here to there," we may liken it to a somersault. The movement which carries a somersault is initiated from a spring, reaches a peak, turns the force, and balances in its completion. Tiny somersault cycles are necessary to extend the leverage up and down the keyboard.

Excluding the extension of the torso and top arm, the blended action proceeds when the radius is allowed to twist over the ulna (the two bones in the forearm which articulate just below the elbow joint) and continues through the pinpoint axis of interaction through the wrist. The slight movement in the forearm which causes rotation carries the closely adjoined hand, wrist, and fingers as a unit. The thumb, as part of the total unit of rotation, follows and swings close to the axis of the hand. In fact, the thumb and the last finger to be played feel as though they were extended from the center axis in one piece. This close association to the axis eliminates lost movement when the direction of the somersault is reverse in its cycle.

These tiny somersaults occur innumerable times within the ongoing long lines of progression up and down the keyboard without disturbing the total rhythm. If the thumb is reaching ahead, or if any movement is shut off or occurs out of proportion, there will be bumps and jerks, and the playing will be less than continuous.

As a step in sensing wholeness in an ongoing progression such as an arpeggio or an extension, the pianist should allow his arm to lead the last finger played off the key and should suspend the entire arm in the air just above the keys. The performer must sense the gravitational pull through the body to the chair, and should sense the arm resting in this force. It is then possible to feel the arm making the slightest plunge downward as though it were falling. Quickly, however, it completes a circular somersault through the wrist and forearm and finishes itself on the first finger of the new pattern, usually on the thumb. Balance is sensed between the last finger played and the new finger. Students should do this exercise in the air until the movement is perfectly blended. As one becomes more skillful, the movement becomes smaller and smaller through the diametric axis. In fact, it is no secret that one can scarcely detect this movement at all in the artistic performance.

In scales, the same principles apply, but the patterns are very much smaller. The balanced center supports and carries the periphery, and the tiny adjustments are smoothly "tucked into" the total rhythm.

Skips and extensions of patterns in any direction should be sensed through the interaction of the two forces. Just before the extension into a new pattern, one senses himself traveling upward in the new wave. The tiny breath impulses assist in the "down, up, and over" cycle.

SMALL ADJUSTMENTS IN ARPEGGIO
AND SCALE EXTENSIONS

The ease with which one executes pianistic patterns is usually associated with facility, speed, and brilliance. As necessary as it is to be uninhibited in such demands, it is equally and sometimes

This student senses the pull of gravity as he rests in the split second before performing the "somersault" in the arpeggio.

This student is feeling the hand as a unit, thereby eliminating the feeling of unrelated fingers. There is an exaggerated "screw-driver" twist through the two bones of the forearm before minimizing the tiny rotation in the somersault.

The thumb as a part of the hand unit follows the line of the dynamic axis through the arm and hand. In extending up the keyboard, the arm and hand move forward while rotating slightly to the right to initiate the somersault. Rotation will be completed when the two bones in the forearm swing to the left in balance. The thumb is ready to receive this direction.

more rewarding to be in tune and to respond organically to the realm of more slowly moving melodic and harmonic tendencies awaiting resolution. This is the area in which the true musician searches, experiments, and weighs the possibilities of enhancing his "tone-touch palette" in order that he may satisfy his perception from within and ultimately serve the musical significance by mastering his instrument. When the image is clear and the desire is intense, the neuromuscular response through experience and habit will move the leverage in relation to the keys to create the desired tone.

TONE QUALITY

Many pianists cannot understand why different artists playing the same music on the same instrument in the same auditorium create tones of different quality. We make no pretense of understanding this phenomenon, but will list a few findings.

Tone quality can be influenced by two major conditions. The first is the instrument, and the second, the pianist. Surely everyone will agree that any performer cannot hope to experience the same quality of tone from an old "clunker" that he does from a nine-foot Steinway. The condition of the piano is of the utmost importance, as are the acoustics of the hall or room.

The pianist's knowledge and experience with the possibilities of primary and partial overtones in the different registers of the piano also contribute to tone quality, however. The skill with which the performer uses the pedals singly and in combination, sustaining and releasing the desired and undesired vibrations, affects quality.

Through science, we learn that amplitude and pitch do not affect tone quality. Tone quality depends upon the manner in which the string is put into vibration; in other words, tone quality is directly dependent upon dynamism. As stated by Dr. Hermann Helmholtz, tone quality depends upon the way strings "begin and end."[2]

---

[2] Hermann L. F. Helmholtz, *On the Sensations of Tone As A Physiological Basis for the Theory of Music* (New York, Peter Smith, 1954), p. 19.

Again we come face to face with the fact that the content of form determines the organization of the energy of the carrying-line. The rhythmic curvature directs the inner action of the individual tones as one goes into the key action and comes out of it. "Exciting a string," as Dr. Helmholtz calls it, is in direct relationship to the desired tone quality which the performer perceives as necessary to the fulfillment of the musical content. Pianists often refer to this degree of velocity as the "ping" of the tone.

In fast tempos, the primary tone or fundamental is more apparent because space and time do not allow the vibrations of the overtones to continue. Of course, in a slow tempo, where rich, deep sonorities are desirable, the performer's sensitivity should cause an entirely different degree of excitement of the string through controlled key action.

In a recital of students, each one, regardless of teaching approaches, has degrees of individuality in his tone quality. It is often said that "your tone quality is you." The vibrant person (one who breathes totally and maintains a balanced, lightweight body with a strong urge to hear) usually produces the most resonance. Physique is seldom a consideration. If the vibrant pianist senses and masters the dynamics of curvature, the individual tone will be distinguishable in its own nature.

X. Strengthening the Concepts

I. THE APPROACH
1. Do I understand the character of the piece?
2. Am I reading all of the symbols correctly?
3. Do I actually *feel* the relative note values?
4. After the first reading, am I using the best fingering?

II. CONDITIONING
1. Is the bench or chair the right height and the right distance from the keyboard?
2. Do I feel alive and in one piece from my toes to the top of my head and to the tips of my fingers?
3. Am I balanced and free to move or turn through the spinal axis? Are the sit-bones rooted as securely in the bench and are they as easy to spin from as the toes of a ballet dancer against the floor?
4. Am I allowing the chair or bench to support me?
5. Do my legs assist in counterbalancing the movement of my torso and arms?
6. Can my legs swing easily to and from the pedals? Do they assist in balancing and in initiating power and impulses when necessary?
7. Am I directing the line of force through my hip joints aligned with the sit-bones to the chair so that I neither spill forward from, nor push against, the pelvis and lower back?
8. Am I disturbing the balance of the rib case through slumping, pulling forward, or pushing against my back?
9. Is my shoulder girdle freely balanced, is my sternum high and floating, and are my shoulder blades flexible but usually folded close to the center?

10. Are my arms free to move but snugly centered in the shoulder sockets? Are they supported through the two forces in the center? Are all movements initiated and completed through the center axis?

11. Are the knee, shoulder, elbow, wrist, and finger joints free to move within their natural functions?

12. Are the repetitive, rotational, and undulating movements in *rhythmic* proportion to the keyboard articulations?

13. Does the line of force through the axis of the arm connect and open the hand span correctly?

14. Are the bones of the fingers connected through the joints and are they firm enough to transmit to the keys? Is the energy blocked by pushing upward against the hand-knuckle joints?

15. Does the merged action of rotation and undulation complete the spin through the fingers and thumb?

16. Do the arms, hands, and fingers remain vitally connected through the use of the connective tissue groups during and between patterns?

17. Is the thumb free to rotate from the joint adjoining the hand? Does it connect to and function in the arc of the whole hand?

III. PREPARING TO PLAY

1. Is my mind's ear imaging and sensing the tempo and the rhythmic carrying-line, inclusive of the motive, measure, and phrase?

2. Do the mind and ear relate to the feel of the shapes of the patterns on the keys?

3. Am I holding back, lifting up, or pushing ahead of the rhythmic line?

4. Is the "imp" in the impulse fast enough to turn the motive, measure, or phrase?

5. Am I making a smooth transition from impulse to suspension?

6. Are there dead ends in my movement, either in the total rhythm or in the timed patterns of articulation?

"Now."

Not enough "imp" in the impulse!

Can I play without my eyes on the keys?

7. Am I breathing deeply enough to vitalize the accessory muscles of the pelvis to support the playing process?

8. Am I allowing the breath to assist in initiating the impulse, resting in motion, and sustaining the suspensions?

9. Am I sufficiently quiet and are my forces sufficiently organized to serve the total playing process while releasing the meaning of the music?

10. Do I have to think about these reminders when playing a composition in a performance or for my own enjoyment? *If so, I need to learn the habits until no conscious thought is required.*

There is always the student who has a very keen intellect but who is so focused upon mechanical detail that he loses the sweep of the whole. He "thinks" only in partial readiness and therefore does not "feel' in wholeness. There is no vitality in his pulse. However, if he is assigned a research project to observe the interaction which produces the curvature of the two forces evident in all nature (such as the rings in the old tree trunk or the pebble thrown into the water or the water leaving the bathtub), he may be able to convert the imagery into the playing experience. The quick, sit-bone-directed breath impulses, the spring from the bench to the feet, and the octave exercise are but three of the stimuli to awaken motion through the feeling of wholeness.

At the other extreme is the student who, usually with a very good ear and a reasonably fine mind, yanks, jerks, and grabs ahead of the organized center control. His desire to hear cannot wait for the rhythmic follow-through. Again, stress is placed on the balance of the forces in center, but for a different reason. Through channeling this explosion through imagery of "always starting in center," habits of stability replace habits of disorganization. This type of student is very often what teachers call "talented." His playing is usually spirited but uncontrolled. This kind of student should "bop" with the breath on every note value and deliberately slow down the curve at the end of the measure motion. This approach usually results in satisfying improvement for the "eager beaver."

There also is the somewhat confused transfer student who may have been habitually drilled in a weighted technique. His concept of starting with his hands is highlighted by striking a blow on count one as the "strong beat" and by progressing "in strict time" with slightly less weighted "weak beats." He is completely devoid of any feeling of wholeness of motion or of suspension. This is the student who may have changed teachers because he realized something was lacking and who has made up his mind that music is not at all what he originally thought it was. With great patience, the teacher can gradually lead him into the feel of large patterns which are carried through impulse-suspension rhythms. Pictures and imagery of large-patterned sport activities might appeal to the student and perhaps will awaken the imagination. If he is musical, he will no longer like the heavy, unmusical sounds he makes.

It is a formidable task indeed to assist some adults to sense feeling in a one-piece, lightweight body. People, especially adults, who are habitually "swaybacked" and, on the other hand, those who normally sit on their lower backs instead of on their sit-bones, are among those with more serious problems. The teacher should ask such a student to place his hands under his sit-bones, which have been drawn close to center. He should feel the lift through to the top of his head. The teacher can give him the security of the opposite line of thrust by placing his hands on the student's shoulders. The student will probably need help in sensing the centering of his rib case and head. This procedure should be alternated with exercises such as hissing and yawning—breathing techniques which assist in freeing inner motion.

Many pianists who appear to be comfortable and who have assumed a "good" posture are really holding with the small muscles. This condition is not evident until they are actually playing. Any emotional anxiety they might have is well concealed. They should be encouraged to perform breathing techniques with as impersonal an approach as possible. The clearer their aural image and their sense of whole motion, the easier it will be for them to "let go with gravity." Their material should not be too difficult. Perhaps they would enjoy communicating with and playing for others who have the same problems as they do.

Happily, there are always those students who can and will play "in spite of" the teaching. All teachers view these students with great joy, naturally, but it is what we can do for the average talent, while appreciating our prodigies, that is now and always will remain vitally important.

XI. A Justification

There is no other way to justify this deviative approach to playing the piano than to review a few of the problems I encountered and the solutions which were strewn across my path as possible correctives. Of one factor I am thoroughly convinced. Whenever and in whatever way one seriously desires help, he is led consciously or unconsciously to the doorstep of the person who can help him. Had I been a musical genius, there would have been no search. It took the wisdom of instructors to alert me to my true needs.

Mine was a typical case. Even though music lessons were a material sacrifice, my mother wished me to have the opportunity she felt she had been denied. I was thus enrolled at a very early age for music lessons. My mother was told, "This child has musical talent," so the first stakes in the creative-academic gap were planted. Accuracy at any cost, neatly formed hand positions, and all *fortes* and *pianissimos* were observed by my first conscientious and charitable instructor. When I was not scared to death, music was something to be enjoyed. My mother believed that I was making progress, but through unavoidable circumstances, the teacher moved away and a new instructor was chosen.

My second teacher relaxed discipline and stressed the beauty of music. I relaxed along with the discipline, and was no longer frightened. My mother, however, was most unhappy. Music and spirit reigned but my playing was distorted, especially at recitals. When I had not sufficiently prepared my lesson, we listened to minuets by Mozart and little bourrées and gavottes by Bach. Occasionally I was met at my teacher's door with, "Have you ever heard this lovely melody by Schumann?" The die was cast; I loved the music.

Music won the battle, but only a genius senses his responsibility to guard his time and energy in order that he may give to humanity in full measure what the Creator has bestowed, and I was by no means a genius. My musical thirst was unquenchable, however, so the search continued, and that, too, has been fascinating.

Eventually, Gertrude Murdough of Chicago graciously accepted me as a student. By this time, the literature was difficult. One day, holding her head in desperation, she exclaimed, "You deserve to play well! What you need much more than a music lesson is to know how to organize and release what you already have inside." As was her nature, she let no time intervene. She walked to the telephone and called Cora Belle Hunter, whom she knew had studied directly with Mabel Elsworth Todd.

Miss Hunter, along with her love and concern for people, possesses a remarkable gift for detecting blocked energy in the human body and can easily apply this gift to the aesthetic experience. She, too, accepted me as a student, and the mechanical-artistic forces of my musical life were moving toward balance. Motivation was running high, and I was willing to try anything that would hasten a truly musical performance.

What might have been for some the ivory tower of experimentation in performance alone became for me the busy studio of music. The studio proved to be the best laboratory life could offer. Problems, problems! The need to free muscles through the balance of the bones in order that pianistic patterns might be supported, centered, and timed within the musical form became not an hour's but a full day's and often an evening's adventure.

Music became a "calling" and required a dedication to balance motivation. Imagery was shared between student and teacher as a means of awakening the understanding of kinesthetic awareness of organized rhythmic impulses. Symbols became flashing signals of related sounds, time measurements, and dynamics. Tactile memory functioned as scales and arpeggios pyramided in ascending and descending passages. Vibrating trills and chords of all shapes and colors accompanied melody as the outer garmenting of a rhythmic curve. My goal was to fill the storehouse of my subconscious in the service of music. Each day I met numerous people with differing temperaments, and music as one of life's most illuminating experiences now brought the joy of personal response.

Returning to the needs of personal growth, I soon realized that the skill of controlling an outer carrying-line of movement synchronizing all of the elements in the life of music is not enough unless one's feeling arouses an intelligent use of the breath of life to vitalize the total being. Ezekiel knew this, and I was to come to know it. Out of the gift of feeling which nature had given me and which usually resulted in "tenseness," I was privileged to become knowledgeable and to experience "intensity" in proper proportion to the musical meaning.

Along the way, the seminars given by Dr. Maier enriched the balance of my musical experience. Dr. Maier more than generously shared his deep love for the literature of the great masters.

Describing a process is not necessarily finding the reason. To know the reason is to experience the process. Let us not find ourselves in the same plight as the girl who answered, "I didn't know I was studying music. I'm taking piano lessons." To be sure, the instructor's intention was not to separate the academic from the creative. The imbalance can be met with the discovery that at the point where reason wavers, we enter the marvelous stage of wonder through music.

One cannot be wholeheartedly involved in an aesthetic experience without at least partially discovering a philosophy to sustain that experience. Dr. Frederick Schlieder's unwavering concept of music solidified my own philosophy when he said, "Music is something beyond a state of entertainment, pride of performance, and a cultural environment."[1] "The wonders of music are not in the passage of its tonal life, but in the inner life that begets it."[2]

The musician is now justifiably linked through music with space-time, which is without boundary. Is not the recent phe-

---

[1] Schlieder, class notes.

[2] Frederick William Schlieder, *Beyond the Tonal Horizon of Music* (San Francisco, 1948), p. 7.

nomenon which accompanied the landing of *Intrepid* evidence enough? The "strings of the moon" were set in vibratory motion which scientists describe as "though one had struck a bell," and the vibrations lasted for half an hour. The musician as well as the poet may take his place in declaring the universal principle of the "music of the spheres."

Glossary

Amplitude:
> The force of a tone from the initial impact, and the relative amount of horizontal displacement of the waves cycles.

Articulations:
> The movements of the joints necessary to execute pianistic patterns.

Axis (spinal):
> A balanced, flexible, bony columm (pole) within the torso. It supports and controls the movements of the arms and is the result of opposing forces moving in a vertical direction. It serves as the initiator (from the base) and carrier of a long-line rhythm from toes to head to fingertips.

Axis (through the arm):
> Undulating, rotational movements take place around a balanced axis through the arm. The axis causes movement to take direction in articulations.

Balance:
> The bony structure requires less expenditure of energy when balanced. A dynamic balance results from the balance of the mechanical force (gravity) with the living force. (See "Two Forces.")

Ballistic Movement:
> The phase within the rhythmic motion in which the connective tissue groups keep the hand position patterns, the arms, and the torso lightly connected so that they travel in the momentum released in the rhythmic impulses. No one can play skillfully unless this condition exists.

Base of Motion:
> Rhythmic motion initiates structurally from the push against the

resistance of the sit-bones against the piano bench. The muscles respond to the sensed impulse and move the bones. The breath cooperates through the diaphragmatic plunge.

Base of Support:

The lowest points of the ischia bones (sit-bones) are the place upon which the whole trunk weight is balanced in the erect sitting posture.

Blocked Movement:

Improper alignment of body weights causing tensing of muscles. In turn the freedom of the joints is blocked. Blocked movement can result in the body from a faulty aural perception and inaccurate sensing of note values within rhythmic progression.

'Bop":

A sound which lends itself to a quick diaphragmatic bounce. It is easily released and easily repeated. Any other sound that one may prefer is equally good *if* it is bounced from the diaphragm.

Carrying-line:

The synthesization of the elements of the music with the mind-body-feeling of the performer in a geared rhythmic motion which results in an invisible energy form.

Center:

1. An imaginary line in the body through which all the parts exactly balance each other. 2. Any point around which motion rotates, such as the pin-point center in the wrist.

Connective Tissues:

The groups of tissue which connect and aid in stabilizing the body in wholeness. A ballet dancer whirling on her toes needs the connective groups. It is futile for the musician to maintain a total rhythm without using the connective tissue groups.

Cycle:

Movement that returns to its point of origin.

Direction:

Focus of energy in relationship to the center axis from within and its pathway over the keyboard.

Dynamics:

Variation and gradation in the volume of musical sound produced by the release of energy from within the performer.

Energy:

Available power stimulated through imagination; feeling of the motion of the music. Respiration and locomotion generate energy.

Follow-through:

The act of finishing the rhythmic cycle through the channeled pathway within the body, moving from the base of resistance to the keyboard and then returning to the base. The legs assist in the follow-through.

Force:

Strength, energy; potential to be organized.

Fulcrum:

(*Random House Dictionary:* "The support, or point of rest on which a lever turns in moving à body. To make a fulcrum.") The torso functions as a fulcrum for the playing mechanism.

Functional:

Manner of behaving according to nature's laws of motion.

Fundamental Tone:

The generator of a series of harmonics. A simple tone. Harmonics are a multiple of the fundamental tone.

Geared Motion:

Measured motion in rhythmic cycles. Musicians use symbols of measures, phrases, periods, etc. to indicate the desired organization of energy to be released through the body. Geared motion is organized motion as differentiated from movement.

Gravity:

By harnessing this universal force and by keeping our weights in balance, we use it as a tool of support and a base of resistance from which to initiate motion.

Hissing:

Expiring the breath through partly closed teeth, a device for relieving strains by pulling the inner muscles back to center support by lengthening the spine for deeper inhalation.

Impetus:

"Imp" in the pulse. A force which overcomes resistance in motion. A spurt forward.

Impulse:

A stress, a throb, a push which initiates motion in rhythm. A phase in the behavior of rhythm to release the sensed, stored energy in an ongoing flow. Musicians often refer to this experience as a strong beat.

Kinetic Energy:

Kinetic energy results from motion. A musician uses kinetic potential in the ballistic, suspensatory phase of playing.

Kinesthesia:

Awareness of the sensation of movement in the body. This awareness in response to concepts is used as a learning tool in the relationship of the parts to the whole in movement and also in the organization of the motion of the total rhythmic cycle.

Lever:

The musician-pianist is concerned with the levers in the body functioning as a "system of levers." One lever connects with another through balanced bones, muscles, and tissue as the rhythmic line of energy moves from the base over the keys. The spine serves as the great lever, and is adequately equipped with the requirements of a lever, such as a fulcrum, point of resistance, and application of force. The small levers fall into place in the service of the all-encompassing rhythm through the center lever.

Life Force:

The substance of which music is formed. Emotional, mental, and physical factors generate the life force.

Life Forms:

Music which is invisible must be imaged and felt in motion to give it form. It depends upon life's processes for its creation. The rhythmic process moving in cyclical progression results in musical form.

Line of Force:

The pathway by which energy is channeled through the body and over the keys.

Line of Gravity:

An imaginary vertical line which passes through the balanced center of the body.

Movement:

The act of moving usually associated with a movement of a part such as the arm or finger in relationship to the rhythm of the whole. Movement is not to be confused with the motion within a rhythm.

Muscle:

A living engine which serves the musician by moving bones. Muscles also assist in stabilizing. The diaphragm as a muscle serves the breathing system.

Pitch:

The high or low in the relationship of sounds.

Pole:

An imaginary axis balanced through the center of the body.

Potential:

A person's innate ability to respond emotionally, mentally, and physically to musical stimuli.

Relaxation:

Result of a condition which involves the least expenditure of effort. Emotional, mental, and physical balance contribute to establishing a feeling of relaxation.

Rest:

A condition to be sensed. The feeling of being supported at the base (on the bench). The feeling of resting in the balanced motion within the rhythmic cycle.

Rhythm:

Measured motion created of the substance of the behavior of energy. The energy is organized into cycles which move in an ongoing progression. The performer senses the phases as gathering, releasing to a peak, and returning to finish the cycle in order to gather again. Rhythm is a universal phenomenon and is evident in all creative motion.

Rhythmic Line:

Determined by the flow of the music and released through the mind-body-feeling organism in rhythmic motion.

Rib Case:

One of the three main blocks of weight associated with the spine to be balanced within the center line of gravity.

Shoulder Blades:

As members of the balanced shoulder girdle, they aid the musician in achieving a balanced playing mechanism. When close to the spine, they aid in stabilizing the free motion of the arms.

Shoulder Girdle:

Can be likened to a bridge linking the torso with the arms, hands, and fingers, i.e., the playing mechanism. Flexibility and stability in this area are necessary.

Space-time:

A concept to be sensed in rhythmic forms. Total rhythm is a sensed space-time experience. Articulations are sensed in filling space-time forms.

Spin:

Motion which results from "push" and "pull" around the spinal axis initiating from base and completing through the fingertips on the keys. This motion is very evident when we observe a fine artist play a waltz.

Spine:

Vertebral column within the body which serves as an axis of support, flexibility, and balance. As it serves the musician, it gives power, direction, and purpose to movement.

Sternum:

The only place where the shoulder girdle attaches itself through bone to the skeleton.

Suspension:

The phase in rhythm which travels in momentum out of an initial impulse. Motion which is completing a rhythmic cycle. The body should be sensed as balanced in a condition of suspension and as traveling in suspension when finishing the rhythmic cycle. To sense suspension, one is supported through the balance of the two forces.

Symbol:

The sign upon the printed page which represents sound, motion, dynamics, touches, etc., to the musician.

Symmetrical Living Balance:

In designing the human body, nature logically adheres to the functional balance of the life force, which results in symmetry.

Tempo:

Rate of speed of the geared motion.

Time:

The measurement of the individual note values and rests in the metrical units.

Timing:

The space-time necessary to move from one location on the keyboard to another, e.g., from a low base to a chord. The timing of the body motion from impulse to fullfillment of the rhythmic cycle. Adjustments within the tempo-time articulations.

Tone Quality:

"Musical quality of tone depends solely on the *relative* force of the partial tones."[1] The pianist's concern should be to sense and image the necessary energy to be released in the intertonal curvature of the rhythm.

Two Forces:

"Throughout the entire bodily structure run two forces: the one is mechanical, operating on all parts of the body in the same way that it acts on any similar combination of weights, levers

---

[1] Hermann L.F. Helholtz, *On the Sensation of Tone as a Physiological Basis for the Theory of Music* (New York, Peter Smith, 1954), p. 120.

and supports; the other is the Living Force exerted by the neuro-muscular mechanism." [2] The musician moves the bones in order to articulate over the keyboard, and if he moves easily he moves in accordance with the principle of natural balance. The two forces must be balanced through the center to free the playing mechanism.

Undulating:

A flowing movement of adjustment through two or more connected levers through the joints to the forearm, through the wrist to and through the arch of the hand. Wavelike movement through the joints. This wave should not be out of proportion to the rhythmic whole.

Weight:

We do not think in terms of weight. Through imagination and kinesthesia, we think and sense timed movement of the body in geared motion. Through the laws of balance in motion, we channel energy and sense weightlessness in a continuous rhythm.

Yawning:

A diaphragmatic plunge which lowers the vital center of breath. The diaphragmatic muscle assists in vitalizing the rhythmic loco-motion in the sensed time-space impulses. The body follows in a timing that is set by the energy impulse through the diaphragmatic muscle.

---

[2]Mabel Elsworth Todd, *The Thinking Body: A Study of the Balancing Forces of Dynamic Man.* (New York, 1937), p. 41.

Bibliography

Bonpensiere, Luigi. *New Pathways to Piano Technique: A Study of the Relations Between Mind and Body with Special Reference to Piano Playing.* New York, 1953.

David, Hans T., and Arthur Mendel, eds. *The Bach Reader: A Life of Johann Sebastian Bach in Letters and Documents,* rev. ed. New York, W. W. Norton, 1966.

Helmholtz, Hermann L. F. *On the Sensations of Tone as a Physiological Basis for the Theory of Music,* 2nd ed. New York, Dover Publications, Inc., 1954.

Langer, Susanne K. *Feeling and Form: A Theory of Art.* New York, Charles Scribner's, 1953.

Meyer, Leonard B. *Emotion and Meaning in Music.* Chicago, University of Chicago Press, 1956.

Saarinen, Eliel. *Search for Form: A Fundamental Approach to Art.* New York, 1948.

Schlieder, Dr. Frederick William. *Beyond the Tonal Horizon of Music.* San Francisco, 1948.

———, Class Notes, 1944-1952.

Schnabel, Artur. *My Life and Music,* ed. Edward Cranshaw. New York, 1963.

Sinnott, Edmund W. *Matter, Mind and Man: The Biology of Human Nature.* New York, Atheneum Publishers, 1957.

Stein, Erwin. *Form and Performance.* New York, Alfred A. Knopf, Inc., 1962.

Thompson, Clem W. *Kranz Manual of Kinesiology,* 4th ed. St. Louis, The C. Y. Mosby Co., 1961.

Todd, Mabel Elsworth. *The Hidden You: What You Are and What to Do about It.* New York, 1953.

———, *The Thinking Body: A Study of the Balancing Forces of Dynamic Man.* New York, 1937.

Wells, Katharine F. *Kinesiology,* 3rd ed. Philadelphia, W. B. Saunders Company, 1955.

Whiteside, Abby. *Indispensables of Piano Playing.* New York, Coleman-Ross, 1961.

Whyte, Lancelot Law. *Accent on Form: An Anticipation of the Science of Tomorrow.* New York, 1954.

Zuckerkandl, Victor. *Sound and Symbol: Music and the External World.* New York, Pantheon Books, Inc., 1956.